THE
INNER

CW00548937

Work Book

Catherine Summers & Julian Vayne

THE INNER SPACE WORK BOOK

Developing Counselling & Magickal Skills Through the Tarot

©1994 Catherine Summers & Julian Vayne

ALL RIGHTS RESERVED

Cover design by Daryth Bastin

Published by:

Capall Bann Publishing
Freshfields
Chieveley
Berks
RG16 8TF

Contents

by the same authors:

Seeds of Magick
Self-Development with the Tarot
(Both published by W.Foulsham & Co., Slough)

"Time present and time past
Are both perhaps present in time future,
And time future contained in time past."

T.S.Elliot - Four Quartets: Burnt Norton

00 - Foreword

The tarot is probably most widely known as a form of divination, the practice of disclosing the past, present and future of an individual. There are popular misunderstandings and preconceptions of what this practice entails, but most people have an acquaintance with the tarot, if only by sight. Those who have encountered the tarot as a tool for self-development are, perhaps, in the minority but whatever use you choose to make of the cards it is difficult not to learn from them.

In this book have brought together the divinatory and exploratory uses of the tarot. We have explored the two faces of the tarot as separate poles and, where applicable, together. The Inner Space Work Book provides a 'map' for the journey of self-exploration. It may be followed in a variety of ways and whilst the format is that of a workbook, it is written as much for the seasoned practitioner as for the interested, even if sceptical, beginner.

We hope that it will provide you with information by which you will formulate your own ideas. The Inner Space Work Book comprises the views of two individuals on what is a complex and personal subject: none of our words should be taken as being 'the truth' for you, experience is the ultimate teacher.

Finally, it is important to realise that by reading this book you will attain nothing - it is intended to act as a catalyst to action: a key that may help you unlock your own magick. The information and methods given here are designed to act as stage scenery; like any props they are useless unless animated by the actors. Only experimentation will allow you to vivify this book. Only you can give life to the tarot within you.

0 - Introduction

How to use The Inner Space Work Book

This book is intended to be used as a workbook. Each chapter contains theoretical and practical information, and a series of exercises for you to put into practice. There are two paths which may be followed through this book.

The first path will guide you through the basic structure of the tarot and provide you with the necessary information and practices to develop skill in tarot divination. If this is your first encounter with the tarot then you are advised to take this route. Each chapter dealing with the divinatory aspects of the tarot is indicated by the use of the pentagram at the top of the page.

The second path is most suitable for those who have had some contact with the tarot as a system of divination and wish to use the tarot as a means of self exploration. These chapters are indicated by the use of the Unicursal Hexagram . The sections marked with the symbol for Spirit deal with ideas which are pertinent to both paths, and contain a series of evaluation exercises for travellers of either road.

Pentagram   Unicursal Hexagram   Spirit

The History of The Tarot

The history of the tarot is obscure. Experts conflict in their views on the origination of the cards. The earliest existing pack dates from the 15th century, though esoteric doctrine holds that the essential symbolism of the deck is far older than this. Indirect evidence for this comes in the form of the interrelation of the tarot to the Qabalah of Hebraic occultism and subtle coincidences of symbolism of the deck in earlier occulture. Whatever the truth of these matters there is ample evidence that playing cards existed in the middle 1300's and it is not such a wild supposition that these games grew from a degeneration of the tarot system. We have certain evidence in the form of a 16th-century document ('Sermones de Ludo Cum Aliis') that by this time the Major Arcana (that is the main 'picture cards') of the deck were established. The ultimate origins of the tarot are unimportant. Today we are presented with a system of images in the form of cards which interconnect with vastly ancient esoteric systems of learning. Moreover, the cards provide us with a tool for divination and self- exploration that works - this is all that matters.

The first wave of the present magical revival began in the 1800's, primarily with the British based occult group known as The Hermetic Order of The Golden Dawn. It was the sons and daughters of the Golden Dawn (MacGregor Mather, A.E.Waite, Dion Fortune and Aleister Crowley) who brought together the strands of knowledge that comprise the tarot as we know it today. They began the evolution of the tarot as a system of divination and self exploration, demystifying it and fertilising the age-old elements within its structure, so that new growth could flourish.

The Golden Dawn saw the tarot as a method of developing the self, with divination as a side-effect of that development. They reconsecrated the notion that the cards provide a map of the universe, both internally and externally. The tarot began to be seen again as a cyclic system; containing within itself all things. This view is exemplified by Mathers' analysis of the word 'Tarot', written in 1888 (which, incidentally is pronounced 'taro', without the final 't' as the word has a French derivation). The word tarot was given various permutations as follows.

Tora - law or holy book (Hebrew)
Troa - gate (Hebrew)
Rota - wheel (Latin)
Orat - to speak, argue or entreat (Latin)
Taor or Taur - Egyptian goddess of darkness, pregnancy and silence (Tauret).
Ator or Athor - The Egyptian goddess of joy, birth and love (Hathor).

The final 't' in the word represents the fact that the tarot was a cyclical system, not a finite series of cards. (This cycle is depicted in some of the more esoteric decks where the 'first' card 'The Fool' is seen carrying a knapsack full of coins which links him directly with the 'last' card - the Ten of Disks.) The initiates of the Golden Dawn introduced the

3

forerunners of the modern tarot decks (in the 'Rider-Waite', 'Hermetic' & 'Golden Dawn' decks). Crowley pruned back the symbolic 'dead wood' which others left intact, allowing the tarot structure to display the new developments in magickal thinking.

Since the second wave of the revival of the 1960's the use of the tarot has become ever more widespread. Many new decks have been designed and published. Tarot Courses are run through established colleges both in the USA and UK and many Western nations support a healthy number of people who use the tarot for divination on a professional basis. Second only to astrology, the tarot has become one of the most acceptable faces of modern magick with more and more people foregoing prejudice to examine just what lies at the root of this subject.

The Tarot Here

There are hundreds of differently designed decks available at present. Their designs range from cartoon style images to highly esoteric interpretations. There are also many books intended to act as companion texts to particular decks. In this book we have elected to standardise our terminology by using one set of titles for the cards, the suits and a common form of numbering the cards. We have taken as our model for this the Thoth Tarot produced by Aleister Crowley and Lady Frieda Harris, published by U.S. Games Systems Inc. (We have also included the 'Hermetic titles' given to each card as ascribed by The Golden Dawn.) As far as the pictorial symbolism of the cards is concerned we have kept this to the bare minimum for, paradoxical though it may sound, the visual symbolism of the cards is their least important element! Use whatever deck you wish, you need not keep to any choice proscribed by us.

Selecting a deck is of such great, and personal, importance that it is better to omit conscious analysis and rely on unconscious attraction (many people start out with one of the more 'popular' decks and outgrow it. They may then wish to seek out a more profound depiction of the symbolic images or may even feel happier exchanging a tarot containing complex imagery for one with more immediate vibrancy). Try to avoid cards with particular mythos while learning the Tarot or choosing cards with obscure images as this only makes the learning process more difficult.

Go to a shop which stocks a good range of decks (this may be done by mail order but seeing the cards for yourself is better. A 'good' deck is one that resonates with you. It should have evocative pictures, be of a size you are happy handling (the full size Thoth deck is quite large and you may prefer the smaller version or another deck all together). Try to avoid decks which carry too much verbiage (often marketed as decks with 'key words'). Such tarot cards are often pressed on beginners but, as will become apparent, cause more difficulties than they resolve. The choice is yours, just as one person finds the paintings of Salvador Dali can almost bring him to tears, while another detests all his paintings; there is no right or wrong in the matter, it is all a question of personal preference. For those unfamiliar with the Thoth pack it is divided into the units common to all tarot decks thus:

Number	Name	Also known as...
Atu 0	The Fool	-
I	The Magus	The Magician, The High Priest.
II	The High Priestess	-
III	The Empress	The Papess
IV	The Emperor	-
V	The Hierophant	The Pope
VI	The Lovers	The Brothers
VII	The Chariot	-
VIII	Adjustment	Justice (often numbered XI)
IX	The Hermit	-
X	Fortune	The Wheel of Fortune
XI	Lust	Strength (often numbered VIII)
XII	The Hanged Man	-
XIII	Death	-
XIV	Art	Temperance
XV	The Devil	The Horned One
XVI	The Tower	War, The House of God.
XVII	The Star	-
XVIII	The Moon	-
XIX	The Sun	-
XX	The Aeon	(The Day of) Judgement
XXI	The Universe	The World

In most tarot decks (not all cards which use the name tarot conform to this pattern, they may be useful tools of divination but rarely have the depth of the standard tarot structure) it is quite easy to see which cards are which, irrespective of the wording on them.

The term 'Atu' used above means 'key', 'trump' or 'house', thus 'Atu VII is the card called 'The Chariot'. These 22 cards, usually numbered with Roman numerals, are referred to as the Major Arcana or simply Trumps. Stuart R.Kaplan, in his book The Encyclopedia of Tarot describes the Major Arcana as "cards [which] depict and create the continuous and ever-changing physical and spiritual forces affecting humanity."

The remaining 56 cards in the tarot, called the Minor Arcana, are numbered and titled in the Thoth deck, as below. They comprise four suits numbering 14 cards in each suite; four 'Court Cards' (from which Jack, Queen & King in playing cards derive), and 40 'pip cards' numbered Ace to Ten.

The names of the four suits from the Thoth tarot are:

Wands   -   Ace to Ten of Wands
Cups   -   Ace to Ten of Cups
Swords   -   Ace to Ten of Swords
Disks   -   Ace to Ten of Disks

The Court cards are titled:

Knight of Wands/Cups/Swords/Disks
Queen of Wands/Cups/Swords/Disks
Prince of Wands/Cups/Swords/Disks
Princess of Wands/Cups/Swords/Disks

It is quite easy to see how each deck displays these divisions, e.g:

North American Indian Deck:

Court Cards:		Suit:
Chief	of	Pipes/Vessels/Blades/Shields
Matriarch	of	Pipes/Vessels/Blades/Shields
Warrior	of	Pipes/Vessels/Blades/Shields
Maiden	of	Pipes/Vessels/Blades/Shields

Rider-Waite Deck:

King	of	Wands/Swords/Cups/Pentacles
Queen	of	Wands/Swords/Cups/Pentacles
Knight	of	Wands/Swords/Cups/Pentacles
Page	of	Wands/Swords/Cups/Pentacles

Having selected your own deck (and perhaps having bought or made a box or square of fabric to keep them in) you can begin. Select your path now!

Pentagram = go to page 11

Hexagram = go to page 8

7

 # - Who Are You?

Who are you? It sounds easy, but do you know yourself? Are you adding ideas to an already predisposed and limited thinking pattern? For knowledge to be absorbed there must be a 'space' in your psyche uncluttered and waiting. Begin with a simple self evaluation:

Take a blank sheet of paper and write a list of statements about yourself. How do you see yourself? How do you suppose others see you? Which parts do you like, which parts do you dislike? Examine and think about your statements. Put a mark by each negative statement. Take another blank sheet of paper and as you learn something new about yourself or lose something from the old list write it down. Add positive ideas, learnt or relearnt from your experiences. (This exercise forms the foundation of the Magickal Diary which we will discuss in the following section.)

It is vital to begin with an uncluttered and open psyche. Introduction to the self, and to the tarot, do not always occur simultaneously, and any associated background in a bodymind discipline (such as T'ai Chi Chuan or Hatha yoga), psychology, or even fantasy role playing games, will aid your development. Tarot is a form of self- discovery based on ideas which predate all modern psycho-analytic forms. The tarot has no limitations, it is not entrenched in any belief system or field of thought. The structure acts as its own 'inner guide', unifying both subject and object; you are an aspect of the tarot, the cards are aspects of yourself.

The symbols within the tarot in its 'classic' form are common to many cultures. They cross linguistic, ethnic and class barriers, finding a common place in all levels of human experience. In the Alchemical Text Mutis Liber it is said of the Major Arcana that "...the Trumps can be viewed as a silent picture text representing the typical experience encountered along the age old path to self realisation". This is true of all 78 cards which exist individually as parts of the whole deck and also feature the cycle of self, viewed from different perspectives.)

To understand the self as a whole you must begin to see the universe as a whole, with the self as the centre intimately related with every other part of reality. The universe exists as an infinite series of cycles, like the imagined concentric paths of electrons round an atomic nucleus. The patterns which these paths generate in relation to each other may be 'frozen' into units of understanding which Carl Jung termed archetypes and which the tarot depicts on each of its 78 faces. To use the terminology of Hermetic Mysticism: 'the centre is everywhere and the circumference (of the self) is nowhere found.'

There are many theories which may be used to describe just how the tarot may be used as a tool for self-exploration. Carl Jung's modern restatement of age old magickal principles is one of the most useful. The term archetype may be defined as "the psychological aspects of biological facts, the patterns of behaviour by which we live and are lived." There are many archetypal forms, they do not have specific limits but blur into each other like shades in the spectrum. Each archetype binds together many, often apparently unrelated ideas under a single banner. They appear in every culture in the form of gods, heroes or even demons, but a single thread - the essential nature of the archetype - may be seen in them all. Thus the archetype of the 'dying and resurrected god' appears in mythology as Christ, Bacchus-Dionysus, Osiris, Adonis, even One Kenobi from the film Star Wars. The nature of the archetype may be read on many levels; From the perspective of the tarot each card can be seen as an individual - 78 people that you must get to know. The archetypes depicted in the cards are intimately part of yourself, representing the various changes in your state and direction. By understanding and experiencing the ideas contained in each card you will be able to use each archetype, or aspect of self, to its fullest potential.

As a technique for self development you will see the cards as individual aspects, in a more analytical light than that required to use them as a divinatory method. In divination the tarot is considered as a whole system, whereas in its self exploratory use each card-archetype must be encountered alone.

Preliminary Exercises:

Write down the points listed in ' how you see yourself' and then write answers to the following questions.

I) Take out your deck and look through it. What cards (archetypes) immediately strike a cord within you? List them. Is there one card which is you?

II) What cards/archetypes leave you cold? List them out.

III) How do you see self-exploration affecting your own life and the lives of others around you?

IV) What do you think will be the most difficult part of your own nature to master or understand?

☆ Tarot Out of Time

The tarot may be used as a tool for divination. Divination proper is not the same as fortune telling. Fortune telling is the humourous, if not always harmless, trickery to be found in the fairground. Nor is divination, when correctly used, the same as the mysterious foreshadowings of fate given by the Oracles of myth.

Divination means the art and science of discovering by organised intuition the past of an individual, their present situation and outlining possible courses of action and possible results of any given course. Divination here does not mean being able to predict the future. With rare exceptions it is impossible for anyone to predict the future with absolute certainty. It is also impossible to describe totally the past or even present of anything. Each of us has a different viewpoint of even the simplest event or object. The use of the tarot does not in any way rely on the notion of 'fate' or 'destiny' as normally understood. The proper use of the tarot for divination relies on a series of ideas as follows.

The first principle is that the tarot may be used as a means of organising the intuition. The cards of the deck have no power in themselves. They are 78 painted cards which, like a set of paints, can only produce a masterpiece when used by a skilled hand. The tarot is designed to stimulate chains of inspired thought; to act as a key which unlocks the clairvoyant ability which is present in all humans. The second principle is that the tarot provides a medium whereby intuitional ideas may be expressed in an objective way. The tarot is a means of gaining and expressing information. In essence it is a means of communication, unlimited by the constraints of culture or even of time.

Before considering the process by which intuitional insight may be gained; how does the tarot reader define the future. The possibilities of individual action in the future may be imagined as running, like fault lines through a crystalline stone, such as marble. In the case of such a rock the sculptor may be fairly certain that a blow will cause the rock to fracture along the fault line, just as wood splits along the grain. There is always the possibility that the rock will split along a smaller fault line, perhaps even a line hidden deep within the rock away from sight. The predictive function of the tarot operates in the same way. The reader may see that the client has four courses of action open. Course A will probably result in situation

A1, course B in B1 and so on. The reader may even be able to be able to ascertain just which course of action the client is most likely to take. In any case the method of divination is, for the most part, qualitative and based on probability. It is probable that a tourist in Egypt will experience warm weather but it must be remembered that there is always a possibility, however slight that, on touchdown in Cairo Airport, the hapless holiday-maker will see snow. In just the same way it may be that unrecognisable factors will result in course A producing situation B1; however as you become more skilled in reading you will find that the accuracy of your predictive skill increases dramatically.

How does it work?

The honest answer to the above question is that nobody is certain. There are a number of theories which attempt to describe the possible mechanics of the tarot. The majority of these attempt to explain the predictive divinatory function of the cards, and, to a lesser extent the way the tarot acts as a tool to provide information on the past and present. Ultimately, it is unimportant just how the subtle mechanics of this tool operate, however the following theory may provide a useful starting block from which to examine your experience and evolve your own ideas.

Carl Jung evolved a theory based on ancient esoteric doctrine which he termed 'syncronicity' or 'the theory of meaningful chance'. Briefly stated, Jung suggested that nothing in the universe occurred just by accident. For example you will probably have experienced curiously repeated events in your own life, you may come across a word which is new to you in a television programme, you may then see the same word written in a book and then perhaps a friend will use the same word in conversation. We tend to put such things down to 'co-incidence', a word which is useful but totally meaningless, for 'co-incidence' side-steps the question 'why?' by saying 'well that sort of thing just happens'. Syncronocity holds that the events in the universe exist like threads running through a complex tapestry. Occasionally these threads become visible above the main body of the fabric of the universe (such as in the case of the new word encountered above). The conscious mind would be incapable of processing all the necessary factors to extrapolate this meaning and so a random system is used to by-pass the conscious mind and allow intuitive responses to well up from the unconscious.

The vital point in the above theorem is that the ability to read relies on the ability to access the unconscious mind and to express the information provided by that level through the conscious. A good reader is able to suspend the self between both these levels, gaining information and then manifesting it in intelligible form. The ability to mediate in communication is your goal. Reading the tarot is not an excuse for giving up ones' own ability to make decisions. The tarot is a guide, a method of disclosing the present and past and allowing you or your client to make their own decisions on the future. When reading for others the tarot provides an unsurpassed method of counselling. The reader may guide the client but always with unbiased neutrality. When reading for yourself, the tarot acts as a way of discerning your own situation and possibilities as well as providing an excellent opportunity for taking an objective look at your own circumstances. In either case, like a road map, the tarot provides you with the lay of the land and potential routes; you have the free will to travel them as you wish.

Preliminary Exercises:

Take a sheet of blank paper and write down answers to the following questions:

I) What do you understand by the term divination? Does your comprehension of this concept differ from the definition as given above?

II) Why do you wish to learn to read the cards? How do you see your development/ability in relation to your own life and that of others?

III) What do you think the most difficult aspect of learning the skill of divination will be?

This exercise forms the basis for your Magickal Diary which we will discuss in the following chapter.

- # Emergence into the Tarot

The learning process is a continuous one, there is no end. Just as there is no perfected 'best' in biological evolution there is only variation, adaptation and change. As you work through this book, entrenched beliefs will shatter and new perspectives and ideas will emerge. In the context of development of any skill (from levitation to playing the piano) the formula expresses the following 'Three Stages of Learning'.

The Isis Stage

Isis is the great mother goddess of Egypt. In the Tarot the Hebrew transliteration of the letter I (yod) is attributed to Atu IX 'The Hermit'; the central symbol of which is the seed.

At this stage you may feel the initial excitement felt when beginning any new project. The novelty of the experience gives a certain zest to even the most laborious practices. The benefits of exercises can be readily felt and your knowledge increases in leaps and bounds.

The Apophis Stage

Apophis is the dark serpent of the desert sands. In the tarot the Hebrew letter is Aleph which is attributed to Atu 0 'The Fool'. The central image here is of one who has lost their way in the desert.

This phase is 'when the going gets tough'. At this point initial enthusiasm gives way to a growing sense of defeat. None of the exercises attempted seem to yield any results and the feeling that the daily grind of practice is 'just not worth it' sets in.

The Osiris Stage

Osiris is the dying and resurrected god of Egypt. In the tarot, the Hebrew letter given is A'yin, linked to Atu XV 'The Devil'. The symbol is of vibrant new growth rising from the sun-scorched desert.

If the 'dry' phase of Apophis can be overcome then the dawn breaks. The Osiris phase occurs when you understand the benefits gained from your past struggles and see your confidence and competence established through 'the school of hard knocks'.

This cycle applies in all aspects of everyday life. It has occurred to you in the past and will occur again. With the disciplined perseverance necessary to learn the use of the tarot, these stages will become apparent. At least, when the Apophis phase occurs you will be able to take some small comfort that, with dedication to your desired aim, you will arise anew, like the mythical phoenix.

Keeping A Diary

A vital part when working with the tarot is the keeping of records. Writing was once considered one of the highest magickal arts. We have Aleister Crowley to thank for insisting that students of magick should keep their own 'Magickal Record'. Crowley realised that an accurate record of an individuals' occult practices, thoughts, feelings and experiences was vital. Moreover he argued that a diary should be as accurate as possible. There is no use writing 'I sat down and beheld the secret of the universe'; however there is every point in recording 'I sat down at 9pm on 11/2/93 and meditated using the technique given on page 89 of The Inner Tarot. I sat in the half-lotus in my living room and felt a calm sensation of relaxation and attempted to visualise a red triangle ...'etc.

A diary will help you judge your own progress (and mistakes!), and will give you a useful record of events to refer back to. You may notice specific cycles in how productive you find particular exercises and may change you routine appropriately. For example you may find some exercises are best conducted in the morning, others at night. Women often keep a note of their menstrual cycle for just this reason (see The Seeds of Magick by us and The Wise Wound listed in the bibliography). Naturally at certain times in the day, week or month you will find that some activities are better undertaken than others. It would therefore be sensible to swim with, rather than against these tides; just as it would be foolish to go star gazing at noon or hope to go apple scrumping in February.

It is advisable to keep a record of events which will influence your state of mind and you moods in general. The magickal diary should also serve as a diary of your dreams; be they 'full length' dreams or just fleeting impressions. Your dreams are, a doorway into your inner mind. They provide a barometer of your inner mental state. They may also throw up ideas which prove useful, providing a new perspective free from conscious analysis. Hence the expression 'I'll sleep on it'.

15

A ring binder format is perhaps the best way to keep your diary. Your diary is the most vital magickal tool you possess. You need not write slavishly in it every day but you must make every effort to keep your record updated. Always write down dreams and the results of your exercises. Keep your diary by your bed so that you may record dreams immediately upon waking. (After a few moments wakefulness even the most vivid dream may be lost.) Dreams may be analysed to provide a profound method of insight into the workings of your unconscious.

You must tread a fine line between personalisation and objectivity when writing up your record. Honesty is the most important quality in your diary: don't just record emotions, experiences or ideas but attempt to look more deeply at them.

You will need to record your feelings, but should also analyse just why you felt a certain way; you must write what events or experiences have affected you and then use the diary to provide a means of planning future action.

If you keep your record well, you will find it the most valuable tool in your development.

Preliminary Exercise:

Start your diary today!

Time and Practice.

"Practice a thousand times, and it becomes difficult,
A thousand thousand and it becomes easy;
A thousand thousand times a thousand thousand,
And it is no longer thou that doeth it, but it that
doeth itself through thee. Not until then is that which is done.
well done."
-Perdurabo, 'The Book of Lies'.

The most common objection to such an exercise programme is often the limitation on the persons time. The answer is that you do have the time, if you get your priorities right. A simple instance of this that it is estimated that an average citizen in Britain watches over twenty hours of television each week, time which could, in many cases, be much better

16

used. People often come home from work, or put the kids to bed at the end of the day, and say 'I just want to relax'. So why not practice a meditation/relaxation exercise instead of vegetating in front of the television with coffee and soap opera?

Aside of the notion of 'spiritual' development, your practice time will give you a chance to spend some time considering only yourself. This 'mental space' is good for your own psychological well being. Learning the art of making time to be you in your life is vital, especially in the bustle of western industrialised society.

The second objection to discipline is that in personal development why should you need to try, if you do what what comes naturally then your 'inner nature' will bloom outward of its own accord? The answer is' yes' All magickal ability is latent potential but like a seed buried in the Earth it cannot emerge until the overground conditions are suitable. Any esoteric exercise programme relies on the fact that only by creating the right environment can your innate abilities achieve their fullest potential. Disciplined practice need not 'cramp your style' anymore than a good art teacher will hold back a student by teaching them the rules of perspective.

Core Techniques

Place & Position. Mastery of the tarot means mastery of the mind and mastery of the mind necessitates mastery of the body. To use the cards, in any context, you must be able to run through a set of mental gymnastics which cannot be conducted properly if you are unable to sit still for five minutes.

To begin with you must consider the immediate environment in which you need to work, a small room is sufficient. It should be as clean and uncluttered as possible, warm and comfortable. The temperature should be moderate, and the ventilation such that the room is neither cold nor stuffy. Try to ensure that you will be left un-interrupted. The room is better if lit by a low amount of natural light or, in the evening, by candle light. Always err on the side of scarcity rather than over abundance; thus if you wish to use incense use light joss sticks or volatised oil rather than the smokey incenses. Your aim is to set up a room where you can be relaxed but alert and free from as many distractions as possible (as you will see later you own mind has enough distractions, waiting for you, without the constant sound of the T.V playing on your ears).

Your BodyMind

For some exercises you will need to sit or lie for considerable periods of time, up to about half an hour, in one position. To facilitate this you should begin by procuring comfortable clothing. This could be a caftan, robe or even a baggy track suit, you may also wish to perform certain exercises naked..

Taking control of your bodymind complex may be done in a number of ways (if you already have a background in Hatha yoga or similar methods than you have something of a head start). For your purposes here the central techniques are; a) control of position (called 'Asana', in yoga) & b) control of breathing (known as 'pranayama').

Posture

There are four basic positions which you may find useful. They are based on Hatha yoga techniques and may be adopted with very little practice. These are:

The God Posture (so called because it is reminiscent of the way the Egyptian gods are shown seated) is the most useful if you have not undertaking any exercises in stretching your bodies' musculature.

Whichever asana you adopt there are two basic rules to observe;

1) Energy flows along the spinal column from, according to occult theory, subtle energy centres within the body. To allow the flow of force to remain even the spine should be kept in a relaxed, but 'straight' position. (There is no need to sit bolt upright and overcompensate for sloppy posture by creating an exaggerated 'S' bend in your spine as you may observe in marching soldiers or gymnasts.)

2) Your head should be tilted very slightly upward. Do not strain your muscles this has the effect of keeping the mind alert). You may also wish to try an old yogic 'trick' to assist your concentration: allow your tongues' tip to rest on the back of your upper set of teeth, this cuts down the flow of saliva into the mouth and will lessen the need to swallow.

Shiva Asana

Half Lotus

God Posture

Thunderbolt

You should keep your stomach empty of food while engaged in inward-looking exercises. Digestion is an energy consuming process tending to engender drowsiness. If you are going to use any exercise dealing with posture don't eat anything for four hours before practice and limit yourself to drinking water or light fruit juices. It is also wise to empty the bowels and bladder before practice.

The essence of good posture is the ability to remain relaxed and alert simultaneously. This idea is very difficult to convey, especially when we tend to think of the relaxed state of bodymind and alertness of bodymind as polar opposites. If you want to know more consult some of the books on yoga, meditation and posture in the reading list; or watch how a cat can remain poised ready to strike yet motionless for a long period - maintaining a supple tension.

Breathing

Breath occupies a remarkable position in human physiology in that, after only 3 minutes deprivation of oxygen, the systems of the organism begin to fail. As breath is vital to life so it is vital magickal technique. Controlling your breath will allow you a simple key to gain (or rather reclaim) various abilities.

1) The understanding that there is no such thing as an unconscious process. (Breath control does not mean straining to hold your lungs full for 4 minutes just to demonstrate your mastery over your own physionogmy. Rather it means learning to see that you may become aware of, and learn to guide in a constructive way, something you may previously have thought of as a process which your body 'just does'.)

2) The knowledge that you may control the cycle of your breath to affect your mental attitude. (Breathing affects the bodymind in innumerable ways, as well as just keeping the tissues fed with oxygen - ask a mother about how breathing played a vital role in her labour, both relaxing and stimulating. By studying and directing the flow of breath you will be able to cause your mind to enter a desired state; such as consciously slowing down your breathing when you feel anxious.)

A Final Word

Although the information above about posture and breathing may seem a million miles away from your study of the tarot these techniques should on no account be overlooked. As we have said, in order to delve into the hidden regions of your own mind it is essential to develop a firm foundation. Your body and its senses can be aids in your development or barriers. So get to know them first as allies rather than enemies to be ascetically rejected.

Preliminary Exercises:

I) At any given point in your day, stop and become aware of your posture; how are you standing/sitting/lying? Are you comfortable? Is your weight distributed evenly? Etc..

II) Repeat the above exercise with your breathing; is your breathing regular? Is the whole of your chest rising and falling or just one section (most people breath too much from the top of the chest cavity, inflating only about two-thirds of the lungs capacity)? How does your breathing mirror your state of mind?

- The Centre of the Tarot

The core techniques of bodymind discipline, noted in the previous chapter, are vital aids in developing key methods of self exploration. To begin to explore the mindscape of the self it is necessary to understand that the body is the interface between the inner (microcosmic) and outer (macrocosmic) universes. The various facets of both micro and macrocosmic reality may be recognised as archetypal forces - in this case manifested as the 78 cards in the tarot.

The minds of most human beings contain a ragged carnival of unresolved thoughts, emotions, ideas, information and experience. Before you can begin to adventure into the archetypal nature of your self you must take command of your consciousness; rid it of the rubbish and start to build up a new mentality.

Once again we start with the tools already inherent in our own human nature; our ally here, is imagination. Imagination is often thought of as something illusory, to be swept away to make room for 'facts'. Imagination is at the root of the creative ability that makes both beautiful works of art and computer systems. By organising the imagination you can create a microcosmic reality according to your will.

So begin by learning to focus the mind. This practice is difficult and requires effort and determination but it can be done. Organising the imagination is often referred to as 'visualisation', learning to hold a mental image in the minds' eye steadily. Whilst this term implies the use of sight, it is not exclusive as you will have to learn to hold sensations other than the visual, within your mind. The rationale of organised imagination is, that by learning to concentrate on a given thought you will be able to learn to contemplate the action of thought itself. Many of the exercises given later in this book rely on the your ability to hold one idea in the mind and then to move through it to explore its' essence. Thus, one might hold the mental image of the Ace of Wands and use the visualisation as a doorway through which to travel in order to examine the inner nature of this card.

Start slowly and gradually build up your ability. Remember the three stages of learning; at first you will be happy to know that you can hold the image of the Ace of Wands in your mind. you will soon notice however, that you are only able to hold the image for a few seconds before other thoughts interrupt your concentration, but with practice you master the technique. (Many people try long and hard at organised imagination techniques until suddenly, they are successful. The mechanics of the mind, in this respect, are so subtle that the learning process is not often felt until the result is attained, just as the benefit of physical exercise is not immediately noticed if the programme builds up slowly over months.)

A Word of Warning

These exercises will bring you up against a series of great stumbling blocks.

The human mind craves stimulation and when the flow of stimulus is reduced it tends to become bored. Biologically, this functions as a defence mechanism. For instance; if the mind discerns that the body is in danger, it will do its' best to create a variation in the immediate environment, in the hope of preserving it. In the case of a person suffering from lack of oxygen the minds' last line of defence is to throw the body into a fit. In this way, the mind hopes to create a change in the body's environment which will relieve the problem (perhaps the rapid movement of the body will expel a foreign object from the wind pipe or will rip apart a covering over the organism which is causing the asphyxia). The bodymind complex associates lack of stimulation with incarceration, loss of physical sensation and danger.

Humans, in an industrialised society, have become divorced from the constant, harmonious and holistic stream of sensory impressions present in the natural world. We fail to see the colour of the leaves on the trees, fail to feel the passage of the wind, lock ourselves into moving or stationary boxes so that even the march of the seasons becomes a subject of importance only in the timing of our holidays. At first your boredom reflex will play comparatively simple tricks on you and then more subtle and complicated ones (these tricks of the mindscape are often personified in 'classical' occult iconography as demons which the magickian must evoke and then, by understanding their nature, bind under the control of his will. They are not made slaves but willing servants of a more highly defined purpose. The slave master must necessarily hold one end of the slaves chain. The magickian accepts the demons as part of the self and then integrates then into the single stream of his Will).

These tricks or 'breaks' may be divided into five categories:

1) Physical Breaks

These are caused when the restless mind attempts to increase the flow of sensory input by creating irritations in the body, cramps, itching, gurgling of the stomach, etc.. (An extreme example of this records that people who have spent periods in a sensory deprivation chamber, have experienced all the physiological symptoms of a heart attack, the sensation being generated by the mind alone and not any real deficiency in the cardiac muscle.) These breaks may be overcome by asana and relaxed breathing.

2) Awareness Breaks

You will be exposed to many exercises in which the aim will be to heighten your awareness of the physical world. However, there will be many instances where your 'boredom reflex' will heighten your awareness of your immediate environment in a detrimental manner. You may sit down in your quiet room and become intensely aware of the ticking of the wall clock, or the rumble of the distant motorway, or the sound of rain against the window - suddenly your room will have been transformed from a relaxing chamber to the most disturbing environment on earth. The answer is not to seek out a sound proof cell but rather to practice drawing your awareness from the unwanted stimulation and back to your focus. Perseverance is the key.

3) Day-Dream Breaks

This type of break is by far the most commonly encountered. You may start by holding the mental image of a red triangle, then 'come to' and realise that you have forgotten the red triangle completely and are theorising about the political situation in Eastern Europe or about what you want for dinner! This type of break is "very insidious - one may go on for a long time without realising that one has wandered at all."

There is no easy remedy for this type of break. Perseverance is the solution. You must learn to draw yourself back to your focus each time a divisive train of thoughts arises.

4) Recognition Breaks

Recognise these when you find you have stopped to ask yourself 'How well am I doing?'. This usually demonstrates that you are progressing quite well for it shows that you must have been unconscious for a period.

By 'unconscious' we mean that you were performing the exercise so well, that it was flowing through you, requiring little conscious effort (much as balancing on a bicycle becomes, with practice, an unconscious process). Such breaks rarely cause much of a problem and may be overcome by returning your mind to the desired focus.

5) 'Mystical Illumination' Breaks

Of all the breaks of concentration you will experience, this is by far the most dangerous to the course of your development. These breaks occur when the red triangle of your visualisation dissolves and is replaced by the symbol of the pentagram, image of the god Thoth or white light of Buddahood or similar images. Such occurrences of 'mystical illumination' are the the final weapon in the armoury of the boredom complex. They are dangerous because they are subtle and often mistaken as truth. It is as if the undisciplined mind realises that your are pursuing a course of occult development and so deliberately manufactures a moment of occult insight to fool you into side-stepping the exercise at hand.

Once again, the remedy is to return to the point of your exercise. If you start with the intention of visualising a red triangle then that is what you must do. Don't be put off from your aim no matter how many 'spirits from the vastly deep' arrive to proclaim you the prophet of a new aeon!

Exercises

1) First ascertain just how organised your imagination is at present. Begin with an exercise in visual memory. Turn the page overleaf and look for six seconds at the symbol thereon. Then turn back and answer these questions:

i) What figure is drawn in the centre of the symbol?
ii) How many lines may be seen around the pentagram?
iii) What shape is in the centre of the pentagram?
iv) How many triangles are shown in the symbol as a whole?
v) What shape encloses the whole image?
vi) What unusual symbol is to be found within the whole composition?

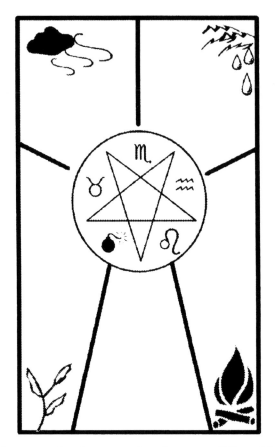

Try testing your visual memory in other ways. What objects have you got at present in your fridge? How many telephones are present in your place of work? What colours was your boss wearing yesterday? And so on.

2) The following exercises provide methods by which you may start to organise your imagination. Begin by seeing just how long you can hold a mental picture. Try three different categories:

i) A simple image, such as to be found on a tarot card, an object such as a telephone or a place such as a favourite spot by the river.
ii) A simple symbol, such as an Ankh, pentagram or red triangle.

iii) A single, uniform colour.

Time yourself with a stop watch. Close your eyes and concentrate. If the image changes in any respect, stop the clock. Note down your results. Experiment with conjuring up smells, sounds, tactile sensations, and tastes as well as visual images.

3) Begin by attempting to hold three dimensional images in your minds' eye. Although these images are more complex we live in a 3D world and it is, in fact, easier to begin with these objects. Record your results.

Try imagining a box. Walk around it, explore its' surface, texture, inside. Make the box bigger and step into it.

4) Try to conjour various sensations into your body by organising your imagination. Sit or lie in an asana in your quiet room and focus your attention on one part of your body, say your left hand. Concentrate your attention on your left hand and experiment with making it feel warm, cool, heavy or immeasurably strong. (This practice is also known as autogenic relaxation and provides an excellent adjunct to self-healing. For example, you can concentrate on a knot of tension in a limb, perhaps visualising it as a blob of red light. Then relax the tension by imagining each muscle slackening and the red area dissolving into a pool of cool blue light.

Getting to Know Them

Having chosen and obtained your deck, how will you get to know your cards?

Just as one meets new friends, is attracted to them, and makes a decision to meet them again, and know them better, so you will need to know the characters in your tarot deck. Each one will emerge as a unique personality. Yet unlike the situation in which you would choose human friends, you cannot divorce any one card from any other (the deck is, in the context of divination, to be seen as a whole, organic unit). If one were to judge a country by one representative, or a conversation by one word, looking at the cards singularly would be misleading. You cannot get to know your deck quickly - you must take time in doing so. The more you observe the tarot, the more information will come to light; and this information will be, of necessity, subject to constant review and revaluation. Take your deck and begin to attune it to your particular aura.

You may wish to keep your tarot in a box or, more traditionally wrapped in black silk.

There are two schools of thought concerning the handling of a deck (which we shall deal with in more depth when considering reading for others). Some hold the view that your cards must remain completely personal (attuned to only your vibrations), whilst others contend that physical contact with the cards need not be limited solely to their owner. Our view is that the cards, like people, should not be kept in isolation. Initially we suggest you should limit the movements of your deck to give you a chance to get to know the feel of them (and to let them get to know you). Keep your tarot under your pillow or with other treasured and personal possessions or carry them with you.

Experiment with dividing your pack into suits, characters - play with them. Look at the characters and ideas depicted. Divide your pack into Major and Minor Arcana and begin with the Major Arcana.

Start with Atu 0 The Fool. This card represents you, beginning your journey; study it!

Before sleeping take out your first card. Keep your magickal record by you - write down your first impressions of the card, anything you notice from closer observation: colour, texture, graphic content. As you progress you will be able to add more information to this list in your diary. You may then evolve an extended character reference for each card. Take a long, last look, and place the card under your pillow, or upright by your bedside. Note any dreams or significant thoughts upon waking. (Remember that you will often get impressions that appear totally unrelated. Record them anyway, there may be a hidden meaning which will appear later, even if it is just that your concentration on the card was weak.)

Repeat this practice with each of the Major and the Minor Arcana cards. You will soon see that your cards form a family, relating and inter-relating, and the beginning of an order will emerge in the deck.

When you feel you are in tune with your deck, and hopefully yourself, attempt a reading for yourself. Don't try to complicate the matter. Keep it simple. Think of something you need to know, perhaps a future event or a clarification of a present situation. Take out a small number of cards. Place them face down and turn them over one by one. (The number of cards, method of turning them and spread are totally up to you, do what feels right and don't limit yourself to what you have read in any book, leaflet or been told. Watch the information emerge, sentence by sentence, to a complete answer. Try this again but don't get into the habit of doing readings. There is no need to look repeatedly and deeply into the cards for a resolution of simple queries, answerable by common sense. If possible, find willing and honest friends who will allow you to read for them. Although we have not discussed particular methods of reading, practice anything you have already learnt. Use your instincts. Don't use a pre-determined spread, watch the fall of the cards and the way they pattern themselves, as threads of the universal pattern. You are both part of this universal pattern and, with experience, may act as its interpreter.

Exercises:

Relaxation and Revealing

Set up an environment as described in the previous chapter, comfortable and free from distractions. To be able to read the cards effectively you must be able to by-pass the conscious mind and so the ability to relax the bodymind is vital. Eliminating all thought from the mind, is supposed to be of great benefit; in many cases this is true but it is extraordinarily difficult and for the purposes of divinatory work unnecessary.

So to begin with just concentrate on becoming aware of your own mental state and allow your conscious mind to relax allowing a free flow of unconscious impression. Lie on the floor in the Shiva asana and just become aware of your own body. Notice any aching or stiffness in your limbs. Let your thoughts come and go as they wish. After a few moments interrupt your chain of thought and try to retrace its' route. Begin with five minutes and gradually increase the duration of this exercise, by five minute increments, to half an hour. (This exercise is worthy of repetition throughout your development. If you perform it correctly you will notice something new every time.)

Experiment using gentle music, coloured lights or relaxing incense and just let your bodymind relax. Experiment with whichever variations of this method appeal to you (perhaps trying to focus your attention on one limb and becoming aware of its position. Then relaxing the muscles of your hand, for example, until it is totally relaxed - then move your attention to another part of your body).

Keeping your Magickal Record

Whenever you perform an exercise, record the results in a detailed form. An example of the style in which you may wish to write down your exercises is given below.

Time: 9.00pm Date: 11/02/90 Place: At home in living room.

Duration of practice: 15 mins.

Objective of Exercise: to discover more about the nature of the Suit of Wands.

Preparation: made the room as comfortable as possible. Removed obvious distractions. No music or incense used. Lowered the light intensity by using two candles. Dressed in my caftan.

Method: I began by sorting out all the Wands suit, omitting the court cards because they contained too much human imagery and tend to dominate the rest of the cards. I placed the 10 cards out in the form of a circle running from Ace to Ten. I then sat in the dragon posture and considered them, looking at the whole group and then each card in turn. I relaxed my breathing to a steady level (about four second breathing in and exhaling for the same period, although I did not count my breathing cycles duration). I then shut my eyes and let ideas come to the surface of their own accord.

Results: I was startled by the range of red tones in the Wands suit. I became very much more aware of the vibrancy of the Wand cards. Even the stable cards, like the Two and Ten still seemed to evoke a real feeling of raw power. After closing my eyes I found that I was thinking more and more about the way the Wands met in the pictures and about what happens when one force met another, both in harmony and conflict; the irresistible force meeting the immovable object.

Summary: I found this exercise very useful, if rather difficult (my mind wandered into areas which I saw as blind alleys, some four minutes, after I closed my eyes). I found my train of thought becoming increasingly visual, probably stimulated by the images of the suit and less like a string of mental words.

Action: I'll try this exercise out with the other suits and then perhaps with other groups, such as the Court Cards. I'll see if using incense helps, possibly a cool scent such as jasmine for Cups and an earthy smell like musk for the Disks.

- The Structure of the Tarot

You will already have noticed that your deck contains a series of subdivisions; the Major Arcana, Court cards and 'pip cards' of the suits, which are four in number. Depending on your deck it may seem that some of these sub-sets are more dominant or important than others; yet to appreciate the beauty of the tarot you must see how these elements interlock to form a whole system.

The tarot is a series of cards which depicts the movement of energy: this flow may be defined in many ways : by the use of Hebrew letters and the Qabala, or the use of psychological terminology or other esoteric constructs. The divisions of the tarot are not arbitrary but mirror the exchanges of energy which occur at all levels within the universe.

To enable any system to encompass the essential nature of the whole universe, that system must treat the universe as a series of interconnected energies. Duality with the tarot is expressed in many ways. The duality between the Major Arcana, which express complex concepts, and the Minor Arcana, expresses the simpler ideas from which these concepts are generated. Duality also exists within the cards themselves, most overtly in the Major Arcana. There is a juxtaposition of life and death (commonly depicted by a 'living' skeleton) in Atu XIII 'Death', or in Atu 0 'The Fool' who combines both genders, also foolishness and wisdom to form a curious androgynous figure.

It is the unit of four through which the structure of the deck may be most easily apprehended.

Within the deck the obvious manifestation of 'the four' comes in the Minor Arcana as the four suits of Wands, Cups, Swords and Disks. The four-fold division is described in terms of the elements, and it is within the concept of element that the doctrine of correspondence is encountered.

The theory of correspondences, which used to be known as the 'doctrine of signatures', is quite simple. It provides a system of 'file headings'. Under these headings, an endless range of emotions, objects and ideas and may be filed. The headings may also be used to describe the 'feel' of the inner nature of anything. Each of the four headings provide a means of linking together and describing any part of the universal whole.

Correspondence is, essentially, a means of communication.

Each suit is attributed to an element thus:

Wands	-	the element of Fire.
Cups	-	the element of Water.
Swords	-	the element of Air.
Disks	-	the element of Earth.

The names used for each element, such as Fire, refer not to physical Fire but to a complex of ideas which may be described as 'fiery'

FIRE: 'having a fiery temper', 'hot-headed', the 'creative spark', 'flaming mad' are expressions which display some aspects of this elemental nature. Fire is associated with qualities such as: passion, violence, lust, generosity, imperiousness, swiftness, unpredictability, spontaneity, recklessness, enthusiasm and ambition. Red is the colour most often associated with Fire. Its gemstone is the ruby, opal or diamond, the compass direction ascribed to Fire is South. The energy of Fire is described as being masculine-positive and is the most active of the elements (and therefore the most unstable).

AIR: 'head in the clouds', 'like a breath of fresh air', 'as swift as the wind' and 'a flash of inspiration'. Some of the qualities associated with Air are: intellect, analysis, unreliability, capriciousness, flexibility, accuracy, penetration, cunning, rationality, dexterity, skill, and wit. Pale yellow and light blue are most often associated with this element The gemstones are topaz, chalcedony, artificial glass and crystal, also the direction of East. Air represents intellect, as Fire represented the basic drives and desires. It is regarded as a masculine-positive energy.

WATER: 'Still Waters run deep', 'wishy-washy and wet', 'his name is writ in Water', 'go with the flow'. The qualities associated with this element are: illusion, emotion, reflectivity, responsiveness, subtlety, dissolution, secrecy, intuition,voluptuousness, indefaticability and indolence. Sea greens and silvers are associated with this element as are the gems of moonstone, pearl and beryl. The direction associated with this element is West. As Air is associated with the intellectual facilities of the mind so Water represents its' intuitional, emotional abilities. Water is described as being feminine-negative.

33

EARTH: 'salt of the Earth', 'solid as a rock', 'rough diamonds', 'in tune with the land'. The emotions and qualities associated with this element are: stability, slavishness, fertility, steadfastness, thoughtfulness, and caution, trustworthiness, materialistic, slow, crystallisation, reticence and kindness. Symbolic of this element are the colours green, brown and black, as are salt crystals, garnets and emeralds. The remaining direction of North relates to the Earth element. Earth is the foundation upon which the other elements act: much as the drive (Fire), intellect (Air) and emotion (Water) manifests through the medium of the physical body (Earth). This element is described as being feminine-negative.

These correspondences are true at many levels and so the umbrella classification system of the elements may be applied to any situation, from describing the mechanics of a car engine to the interplay of emotions between parent and child. The logic of certain correspondences is quite apparent: fire is reddish in colour, and is therefore related to ruby which is a red stone and to the metal iron which oxidises red (rusts) to form the colour of that gem. Others need more thought: red corresponds to the qualities of violence and courage. A biological example of this would be that the colour red stimulates the adrenal glands which prepare the bodies' physionogmy in a combat situation, while historically soldiers, such as the Roman Legions wore red.

One of the most commonly used ways of expressing the interaction of the elements is by the use of the pentagram.

This symbol appears in many tarot decks and throughout magick. With one point uppermost, it represents the notion that the elemental forces are emanations of a force known as 'spirit', while two points uppermost it depicts the idea that through understanding the interplay of the elements, one may understand the nature of spirit. The word spirit is a confusing term, often used incorrectly. Spirit is simply the sum of the four elements combined to produce a harmonious fifth element, much as four chemicals may react together to generate a new compound. The whole becomes duality, which becomes four-fold which resolves back into the whole.

The Major Arcana may be seen as being spirit and the four suits, the elements which generate it. The elemental forces also exist within each Major Arcana card; a common example of this is the depiction of the four 'Kerubs' or figure-heads of the elements in most renditions of Atu XXI 'The Universe'. A human figure is shown surrounded by four animals - a

34

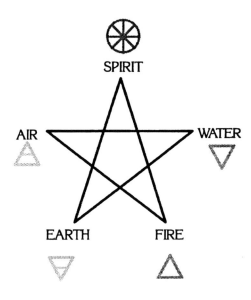

lion for Fire, a man for Air, and eagle for Water and a bull for Earth.

Further divisions exist in the structure of the deck which you may wish to investigate. For example the Court Cards may be described by using the 16 subelements thus:

Knight	Wands	Fire of Fire
Queen	Wands	Water of Fire
Prince	Wands	Air of Fire
Princess	Wands	Earth of Fire
Knight	Cups	Fire of Water
Queen	Cups	Water of Water
Prince	Cups	Air of Water
Princess	Cups	Earth of Water
Knight	Swords	Fire of Air
Queen	Swords	Water of Air
Prince	Swords	Air of Air
Princess	Swords	Earth of Air

Knight	Disks	Fire of Earth
Queen	Disks	Water of Earth
Prince	Disks	Air of Earth
Princess	Disks	Earth of Earth

This system extends the elemental classifications, and describes with more accuracy the nature of each of the forces depicted in the cards. Thus the Queen of Disks represents the Watery part of Earth, symbolising the fertilising force of Water manifesting through the physical matrix of Earth. The Prince of Wands represents the Airy part of Fire, therefore his character could be described as 'sharp', or full of swift, rapacious wit, combining both the intelligence of Air and rapid activity of Fire.

The division of the cosmos into seven (as the seven 'planets' of the ancients: Sun, Moon, Mercury, Venus, Mars, Jupiter & Saturn), and into 12 (as the signs of the Zodiac) also occurs within the tarot.

The point of all these sets and subsets, is that they are intended to allow you to experience the universe and describe it in easy 'bite sized chunks'. The tarot is not a finite series of two dimensional cards but a fabric of ideas, woven in one overall form with infinite skill, relating to you, and others, at all levels of experience.

Exercises

1) Try to discover new correspondences and divisions in your deck.

Lay out the cards in various piles and examining how they interconnect.

As suggested above the Major Arcana may, be seen as the fifth element of Spirit. Alternatively the Major Arcana may be divided in terms of the four elements.

Take the Major Arcana and place them in four piles, one for each element. You will have two cards left over, perhaps cards which hold the elements within them, in such balance, that they correspond better to Spirit than any one force. Try various arrangements and record your results. If you have any knowledge of astrology, you may wish to use this to assist you in this exercise, take care not to simply repeat your knowledge of the planetary and zodiacal forces in the context of the cards.

Look for something new!

2) Take a large piece of paper and divide it into four columns, each headed with the names of one of the four elements. Under each heading list as many things as you can that partake in some way of that elemental nature. Try as many different categories as possible, but be sure to include:

Colours.
Emotions.
Objects from daily life.
Animals.

Then begin to personalise the categorisations. Think about emotions, people in your life, the various aspects of your own personality. Attribute these to the elements. Use both your logic and intuition. Don't just repeat parrot-fashion anything you may have read either in this book or any other. Analyse why you ascribed each item as you did. Enclose your analysis notes and attribution card in your Magickal Record.

3) Begin to observe your surroundings, and your internal processes, both mental and physical, first in terms of duality and then elementally. Spend a week looking at life through each system of description and keep a note of your results.

4) Evolve your own system of correspondences, or try other forms such as - introvert/extrovert, left wing/right wing or solid/liquid/gas. Experiment with how these divisions need to be extended when they describe qualities rather than one specific state or idea.

5) Select three people in your life and try to correspond them to:

i) An animal.
ii) A plant.
iii) A colour

Then try this exercise with three people who are strangers. In both cases, examine how you derived your correspondences. Are you seeing the features in these individuals in terms of the elements (e.g how they dress, their mannerisms, their personalities and your reaction to them)?

Meditation

This is your first meditation exercise, within the context of this book, so take things easy and don't expect any fantastic results yet.

Prepare yourself and go to your quiet room. Draw a circle on a large sheet of paper and then divide it diagonally with an equal armed cross in your diary. Select a symbol for one of the elements. If you elect to begin with Air you might want to choose a symbol such as a Sword, or the rising smoke from an incense burner. Draw a pictograph to represent your chosen meditational focus in the right hand quarter (the quadrant normally associated with the element of Air). You may wish to use a physical focus, e.g a single candle flame for Fire, of cup of wine for Water. Sit in a comfortable asana and start a regular breathing pattern. Breathe in for a mental count of two (preferably through your nose) and out for the count of two (preferably through your mouth). There should be no straining for breath. This method of breathing is described by the notation 2/2.

Focus your mind on your designated focus and simply contemplate the nature of that element. Allow your mind to drift over the ideas associated with it but pull yourself back to your focus if you begin mentally to Wander from the point. Just see what happens and afterwards record your results.

Repeat this exercise the following day with another element. Fill it in as before on your diagram, and relax using the same asana and 2/2 breathing method.

After four days you will have covered the four elements. So on the fifth night use your completed diagram as your focus. Imagine each quadrant within the circle glowing with a white light as the elements fuse together to form spirit and allow the white light to bathe you in its' brilliance. Once again record all your results.

- Levels of Reality

By now you will have observed some interesting features of your own psyche and the nature of the world around you. Before actively using the abilities gained in the last section, you must begin to consider some rather major philosophical questions. The tarot provides a means of dividing the universal whole into manageable units. Each unit displays the whole within itself, much as a part cut from a hologram will contain all the visual information of the whole.

The key is seeing the reality of the universe as existing at various levels.

The theory of levels suggests that nothing in the universe can be defined except from one view point or 'at one level'. Thus one might say that water is a liquid but this statement is only true 'at one level', that is, when water is between zero and one hundred degrees Celsius, below zero degrees water becomes a solid and above one hundred centigrade - a gas. This is quite straightforward but in magickal theory this principle is carried further.

The tarot describes various levels within its structure. As a means of self- exploration the theory of levels may be used as an aid to examining different strata of reality in both the microcosm and macrocosm. The tarot cards can be used as 'door numbers' to identify each level and 'keys' to allow entry and progress through each. As with the doctrine of correspondence the tarot may be used to provide a qualitative description of the interaction of these levels. One of the 'simplest' ways to explain these ideas may be seen in the esoteric view of the human mind. The various facets of the mind may be seen as being composed of three levels or 'planes'.

No plane is totally distinct from any other - each plane may be seen as being composed of various other levels (much as the four elements contain the 16 sub-elements within them). No plane is more important than any other (much as one rung on a ladder, or spoke in a wheel is of equal value). All levels are arbitrarily designed to create a complete system but are only usable ideas in the way that numbers are useful, not in themselves but as descriptions of the progression from one state to another (e.g '2' is only real as the integer between 1 & 3.)

Thus the mind may be divided into three levels, here described by units

40

in the tarot and terms borrowed from psychology.

Level	Tarot Level	Psychological Term
1	'Pip' Cards	The Conscious mind
2	Court Cards	The Ego
3	Major Arcana	The Unconscious mind

This map of the mindscape, and the more detailed maps which we shall deal with later, are of vital importance. Such systems will provide you with a way of understanding your inner and outer universe as a series of 'bite size' units, interrelating in much the same way that elemental forces do.

Level 1- the conscious mind is the state that humans believe they know the most about. It is the state of mind you are in now, awake and alert, absorbing information through the text. This part of the mind deals in a language composed of simple symbols - letters and words in a language you have learnt. The conscious deals in mathematical units, words and simple pictures most of which you have absorbed from your environment. Most thoughts are processed in a step-by-step logical way at this level, much as a computer processing information. Consciousness is limited because it can only receive limited information from the senses and can only deal with a certain amount of memory information at any given time. (For example it is almost impossible to hold more than two distinct memories about anything in the conscious mind simultaneously, and as the conscious mind derives its' information about the present through the senses the simple act of closing your eyes effectively cuts out 70% of its input.)

Level 3 is the unconscious or 'deep mind'. It is at this level that archetypal forces reside within us, and it is from this level that dreams hail. The language of dreams in the unconscious communicates almost exclusively in symbols and images.

The unconscious is the reservoir of self of which consciousness, in the everyday sense is but a small fraction.

In the context of your development the most important level to thoroughly understand is level 2 - the Ego. The Ego acts as a sluice gate or doorway between levels 1 and 3.

The ego communicates in a combination of both quantitative (conscious) and qualitative (unconscious) languages. It is this level of the self that you must learn to work with in order to access any realms of the conscious or unconsciousness at will.

In most people, the ego acts as a screening service - limiting our perception to a usable level. For instance as you read this page you are aware, through your five basic senses, of a series of other things in your environment - the sound of a distant radio or perhaps the feel of the book cover in your hands. Internally your body is conducting a series of complex actions, breathing, pumping blood round the tissues, pushing food through your gut etc.. All this information is processed in your unconscious, yet your conscious desire is to read this book and so the ego level filters out any distracting information. Imagine the impossibility of concentration on a simple action if you were totally aware, all the time, or every thing about you!

The problem rising from level 2 is that this screening process can limit you so that you are only aware of a limited range of sensations or elements in your subconscious. For instance, let us suppose that you wish to work with the archetypal force of The Great Mother as manifest in Atu IV 'The Empress'. If you have had a difficult relationship with your physical mother, the ego will attempt to screen this level of the unconscious from your consciousness. This mechanism is a protective one, intended, quite simply, to keep you sane, but to develop further, it is necessary to tempt insanity in the sense that you must learn to access and withdraw from all aspects of the unconscious mind, in order to explore the whole of your mindscape. By using systems such as the elemental classifications you can develop a language common to all levels and then may communicate with all levels of reality within and therefore with reality in the outer.

The theory of levels is also used to describe the existence of various unseen forces in the universe; the 'astral body', 'elemental', 'demonic' and 'angelic' spirits, gods and a host of other entities. Magickal theory suggests that there are numerous forces in the universe, which can not necessarily be perceived by the various physical senses, because they exist at different levels of being. A simple instance of this may be seen in the spectrum of light.

The human eye is able to relay information to the brain based on seven different wavelengths of light which we refer to as the 'visible spectrum'. For many years, it was thought that the seven colours of the rainbow constituted the entire range of lights' manifestation. However since the dawn of the modern technological era it has become apparent that we can only sense, directly, a fraction of the whole spectrum of electromagnetic radiation. Xrays, ultra violet light and infra-red remain invisible to us but we have created machines to measure and utilise these unseen energies. In other words we have found technological ways to interact with these unseen levels of reality. So if we begin by taking an god force, such as the Ra-Hoor-Khuit, the Egyptian god of birth and the vitality of the individual, we can begin to describe just what this force is, and how it may be used.

A god exists as the personification of an invisible force. Such a force may manifest itself as the growing of plants or the psycho-physical processes of conception, gestation and birth and it is from these observable aspects that the nature of the force may be discerned. By using a personification, we can begin to see the visible manifestation of the invisible power in both the micro and macrocosm. The 'reality' of a god depends on the perspective from which it is viewed; thus Ra- Hoor-Khuit is real as the representation of the rebirth of life in the Spring season, 'he' may be seen in psychological terms as the vibrant individuality of the rock star on stage, or in a sexual sense as the fiery drive of the individual towards union with another human unit. The elements, gods, angels, demons, archetypal forces of any form provide 'key personalities' within which we may define a certain set of forces within the cosmos.

Where you are dealing with unseen forces in the guise of 'key personalities', you must adopt something known as 'The Special Attitude'. It is this paradoxical attitude which confuses most people about whether or not a magickian believes in 'god' (or 'the gods' for that matter). A magickian can quite happily see Ra-HoorKhuit as a 'real' deity, existing independently and in the next breath describe Ra-Hoor-Khuit as an arbitrary personification of the self - defining the same god as an archetype. The rationale of the Special Attitude is simply this; it may be true, philosophically speaking, to say that any other person is just a projection or element of your self (after all you only know that they are real by the use of your senses which are limited and easily fooled).

However in order to a facilitate communication between yourself and another human it is advisable to assume that they are independent

43

objective, units. So the forces within the tarot may be seen as aggregates of your whole self when using them. You must be able to deal with the archetypes in the deck as subjective units of self, use them as if they were objective entities, and then return to analysing your results as if the force dealt with was part of yourself. The aim of entertaining this paradoxical viewpoint is, ultimately to see that there is no real duality of subject and object, but rather that all things are one. This understanding comes with practice and is an idea to understand by experience and not a view to be held as an abstract, philosophical paradigm.

Exercises

1) Begin by considering just how real is real.

Do your friends exist when you are not with them, and are you therefore unable to perceive them physically? Were X-rays only real after we built machines which could perceive them? What exactly constitutes your mind? (To consider this properly think about the following: the body you inhabit now is not the same as the body you inhabited when you were born, tissues and cells die and are expelled from the body which builds new tissues from the energy contained in your food. The only molecules that stay in your body are a minority in nerve cells in the brain. Yet your brain grows too - in the amount of memory you have accrued over years. Are your brain and your mind identical structures?)

Plane	Quality
Level 1 Upper Spiritual	Will
Level 2 Lower Spiritual	Desire
Level 3 Upper Mental	Synthesis
Level 4 Lower Mental	Analysis
Level 5 Upper Emotional	Sensitivity
Level 6 Lower emotional	Reflectivity
Level 7 Physical	Perception

(This system is commonly used in magick, using the seven planets as a 'base number' from which to divide levels of reality.)

3) Select three cards, at random from your deck and write your own character study of them. See the card, not as part of you but as an objective character. Describe how you see the person depicted (don't forget that all cards can be seen as personalities or archetypes, not just the ones with people on them). How do you suppose that person would react in a given situation? How do you feel towards them?

4) Take one of the cards of which you have written a character study and, having prepared your quiet room use it as a focus. Place the card in front of you. Sit in your chosen asana. Begin to build up a mental image of the character of the cards. Animate the personality in your own mindscape, have a conversation with them and see what you can discover about them.

Reading Between the Cards

Having learnt to see your deck clearly as a system, your next requirement is to experience and perceive the characters implied in the cards. In any society, there are leaders and followers, some personalities will seem more important than others. Certain characters will sometimes appear to lead, giving way to others depending on the situation. This does not mean that your deck can do without a full range of cards, both Major & Minor Arcana. In the way in which a language is created we can equate the vowels with the Major Arcana, whilst the Minor Arcana provide consonants. they are all essential to form words, sentences and, ultimately, the story.

In magick, there is no concept of inviolate truth, or 'fact', and therefore you cannot hold fixed ideas on any subject. (Magick being "The Science and Art of causing change to occur in conformity with Will.") In the context of the tarot, no card may be seen as having one set idea or concept associated with it, but is made up of a series of symbols and ideas portrayed in the images of the cards. Reading the tarot is to see and interpret the changes of meaning exhibited in each card, and by its' relation to other cards; just as in a good book, or a letter from a friend, much is read 'between the lines'. The work of the reader is to observe the individual images, to recognise those which are dominant, and then to feel how each image relates to other cards in the spread (and therefore to discern the changes of relationship implied within each individual card and between cards).

You will need to learn to recognise the potential held in the symbolism of each card. (For instance; Atu II 'The High Priestess, whilst mystical and veiled holds the potential to become Atu IV 'The Empress' - in esoteric terms; the Virgin becomes the Mother, in the exoteric; the querents' potential to give birth to her ideas.)

The meaning of each card exists at various levels. For example Atu XIII 'Death' (which the client will almost invariably take to mean physical death) may have many meanings depending on context. The context may be given by other cards or simply by your own impressions. (Just as X in algebra represents an unknown quantity until defined by other influences around it e.g $4+6=X$.) Thus Atu XIII could mean the termination of the clients' previous employment and subsequent 'rebirth' into a new situation

('Death' often implies a great personal change, often with very productive results, initiating a totally 'fresh start' from entrenched circumstances). It must also be stressed that a cards meaning may be, apparently, totally unrelated to the overt symbolism. Your intuition is the key to meaning, not the description given in any book.

Individual cards, particularly those of the Major Arcana, may also describe the interlinking of two or more 'synchronistic threads', as well as changes in state. (A card may act as a reading in itself as well as being part of the whole divination.) Examples of this in their overt symbolism may be found in the 'Alchemical Marriage' in Atu XIV 'Art', or in Atu VI 'The Lovers' - both representing the joining of opposites to form a whole. Within the whole reading, an 'intrinsic' system may be exhibited throughout the deck. Thus the following selection of cards:

Knight of Cups, Sun, Lovers, Moon, Queen of Disks

....could be interpreted as two people united, if your impressions point in that direction, through love. The central card holds the whole cycle of the reading within it (i.e joining together of two elements), while the rest of the cards demonstrate how this process manifests itself (i.e two complimentary forces, masculine and feminine, working towards a mutual point of contact).

The Major Arcana may therefore be seen as 'setting the tone' for most readings.

Significators & Personalities

The 16 court cards within the tarot often make their appearance as aspects of personality, moreover they are often used as 'significators' within a reading. If a court card appears to refer to a personality then it will refer not to a particular individual but rather to a particular aspect of that individual at a given time. Thus a person who is naturally 'Fiery' by nature you might expect to be portrayed only as a Wand Court card; however such an individual could be portrayed as The Princess of Disks if they were pregnant, or The Queen of Cups if their state of mind was particularly confused and unresolved. It should remembered that although the Court cards may represent human personalities they may also represent the personality of a group, a company, society or family; indeed

47

they may not represent a personality at all - your intuition must be your guide. It is also important to realise that the gender depicted on these, or any card, is symbolic, referring to the quality of the energy expressed and not to physical sex. Thus a man could be signified by the Princess of Swords and a woman by the Prince of Disks or Emperor.

In more structured readings (detailed later) you may wish to select a card to depict the client (or yourself) as they are at the time of the reading. Selecting such a card or significator is a fairly simple business although many books on the tarot over-complicate it. There is, for instance, a theory that red haired women with blue eyes should automatically be given the significator of the Queen of Cups. However from the perspective that each cards' gender is symbolic, that your intuition is the most important factor, and that hair dye and coloured contact lenses are readily available, such ideas are obviously meaningless. If you wish to select a significator you would be better advised to exercise your intuition and establish what sort of elemental 'feel' the querent portrays at the time and choose a card that you intuite is correct, on this basis. (If you have a knowledge of astrology you may wish to use that information as a guide also; thus a person with an 'Airy' nature, whom you know to have Gemini rising could be given the significator of The Knight of Swords, or even Atu VI 'The Lovers' or The Eight of Swords.)

Exercises

2) Pick a three cards at random and attempt to correspond them with:
    i)   An idea.
    ii) A colour.
    iii) An event or stage in your life.

- # Evaluation & Evolution

All life forms must evolve - at physical, emotional and mental levels; magick is the process of becoming conscious of this evolution and accelerating its' pace. The concept of evolution is not, as many 'new agers' believe, about 'getting better', rather it is about adaptation, change and re-assessment. It is necessary for you to continuously revise, review and 'renew' your experience. Bearing this in mind, you should work through this chapter; although it may seem to cover 'old ground' There are new insights to be gained by performing even the most basic exercises however 'far' or 'fast' you are progressing.

Try answering the following questions. Write down the answers on a sheet of paper that may be inserted into your magickal diary.

1. What initially interested you in occultism? What are the factors which lead you to pick up this book?

2. What knowledge of magickal matters did you start with?

3. How have your ideas changed or modified?

4. What differences of opinion have you discovered in the use of the tarot. Are there any points in this book which disagree with anything else you may have read?

5. Write down a list of statements about yourself. Divide them into two columns; the first should be the way you see yourself, the second, how you suppose others see you. (If you have already performed this exercise repeat it and then compare your new findings with those you obtained previously.)

Trial & Error

1. Look back over the content of your diary. What patterns or threads of development can you trace through its pages?

2. Look at the results of your meditation exercises. If you are unsure

about any meditation or other exercise you have done repeat it and note any variation in results.

3. How do you see your development influencing your interaction with other people and situations? (e.g has your sense of awareness changed the way you view your job, your family or lifestyle).

After answering the questions above sit down and take a long hard look at the results. Rigorous self-analysis is called for here. Have you really been as thorough and disciplined as you should have been? Have you neglected certain areas of your development to concentrate on others which you find easier or more attractive than others. Have you tried too hard and attempted to run before you could walk? Have you been seduced by the glamourous mystery of matters esoteric and neglected to maintain a scientific attitude? Are you too logical - missing the whole of the matter by focusing on only one part of it? Are you still able to maintain a sense of humour or have you become the 'serious student' who learns but fails to enjoy the learning process? Try to attack your record and your present state of mind from all possible angles.

Questions from Your Deck

Select three cards from your deck (you may wish to do this at random, if so try to make sure at least one card is a Major Arcana or Court Card).

Go into your quiet room and meditate for at least fifteen minutes on your selected set of cards. Consider the nature of the cards using your intuition and whatever knowledge of their essential symbolism you may have picked up. Imagine the forces depicted in the cards questioning you about the course of action you have embarked upon.

Formulate a series of questions, writing them down if necessary, which the force depicted in the card would ask you. E.g:

The Princess of Wands Asks:

Have you accepted what is in print as gospel and failed to question?
Have you become too introspective and shut yourself off from others?
Are you able to study the tarot and to go out with friends and enjoy yourself?

Have you felt daunted by having so much information to learn and forgotten that understanding flows from within and not without?

The High Priestess Asks:

Are you able to feel the changes within you as well as see them in your Record?
Have your studies made you a more broadminded and tolerant person?
Can you maintain a sense of humility, understanding that you are not necessarily better, or more developed than others?
What do you expect to learn from this point onward?
And so on.

Knowledge Evaluation Exercise

As we have explained, there are few true or false situations in magick. There are many ways of looking at the universal forces depicted in the deck, and all views may be valid. However with the information covered in chapter 1 it is (within certain constraints) possible to be right or wrong in answering a question. The following test questions and exercises are intended to test your knowledge of tarot symbolism and abilities. Don't be too concerned if you get the questions wrong - mistakes are the trellis upon which knowledge grows.

Questions and Answers

1. How many cards comprise the Major Arcana? And the Minor Arcana?

2. What is the name of the Trump card Atu XIII?

3. To what zodiac sign, planet or element is the Trump Atu XVIII - The Moon attributed?

4. To what card is the planet Mars attributed?

5. To what element is the suit of Disks ascribed?

6. Without looking draw or name one of the symbols which appears in the deck you are using on Atu XX.

7. The Zodiac sign of Scorpio is ruled by Pluto, which is a refinement of its' old attribution to Mars (before Pluto was discovered) - what metal would you therefore ascribe to Scorpio?

8. What season of the year is linked to Atu III - The Emperor? (Hint: think about Astrological attribution.)

9. Name one of the symbolic colours ascribed to the Knight of Cups, or one of the colours which appears on your deck in this card. Why do you think it is there?

10. Without looking at your deck, draw or describe how the Swords appear on the Six of Swords.

Exercises:

Naturally you should keep a record of these exercises in your Magickal Diary.

Mis-hearing
Over the course of one day note down how many times you mishear or fail to be aware of something being said to you.

In conversation, do you really listen to what the other person is saying or do you just nod and ignore them while you wait for a chance to interject?

Environment Awareness
Pick a part of your environment and write down its features, then go and check the accuracy of what you have written. Write down the items you have in your fridge or on your bookshelf and then go and see if what you thought was there, is really present.

Random Renewal

Select one exercise, at random from Chapter II and do it. Note any variation in experience from when you first performed it.

Meditation

Take up a comfortable asana in your quiet room and spend a few moments relaxing. Begin to draw your awareness inward from the world around you to focus on your own mindscape.

Breathe regularly and slowly. Become aware of the sounds around you, sounds in the street, of traffic passing, the wind against the windows, the distant sound of voices, etc.. Listen to these sounds and then slowly let them pass from you so that they will no longer disturb your meditation. Draw your attention inward to the sounds within your own room, the sounds from the heating system, etc.. Again become aware of these sounds and then let them slip away from your attention. Go deeper and focus your attention on your own breathing, slow and regular through your body.

When you have reached this point, remain there for five minutes and then move your awareness back outward again; first to the sounds in the room and then to the more distant noises.

Try this at least three times over the course of two weeks. You may then wish to combine it with a simple exercise in organised imagination such as the three outlined below.

1. As you move through the three levels of awareness (outside environment, inside environment and bodily environment) imagine an image which follows this process. For example you could imagine yourself to be, or 'visualise' a flower ('traditionally' a lotus or rose) opening as you descend into your self. When your attention is in the body environment, imagine the flower glowing with inner light. As you emerge back into the the awareness of the outside environment let the image of the flower dissipate without visualising its closing.

You could equally imagine a warm, regular flame rising up from the ashes of a fire or whatever else seems appropriate.

2. When you enter the awareness of your bodily environment imagine yourself as a seed, a point of infinite potential. All around you is the blackness of space. Consider that you are an atomically small point, holding all possibilities within, and that you are within an infinite void in

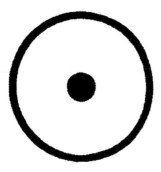

which you can create whatever you will. It may help you to consider the planetary symbol of the sun.

In this symbol you are the central point (or the god 'Hadit' of Egyptian cosmology), within the infinite circumference (The Egyptian goddess 'Nuit').

In magickal symbolism the symbol of the sun becomes the symbol of Spirit, which may be seen as lines of energy interchange existing between the poles of this micro/macrocosmic, atomic/cosmic polarity.

Once you are satisfied that you have covered the first section in this book to the best of your ability, and that you have attained a level of competence, continue with the following chapter.

- The World As Power

In the preceding Hexagram chapter you encountered a series of ideas which attempt to describe the universe. The problem with such ideas is that they may form the fertile ground for philosophical speculation about all sorts of 'big' questions (how can we define reality? Why do we exist? etc.). Such speculation is useful but side-steps the essential purpose of magick - experience. The subconscious mind, and its relationship to the conscious, cannot be understood in the same way that one might understand the equation $1+1=2$, such things must be felt. The Qabalistic maxim points out 'to observe the invisible one must first learn to observe the visible'.

There is a tendency when approaching the whole business of self exploration to become wrapped up in the abstract and to forget and forgo the concrete.

Following the flow of the elemental system you must first get to know the Earth. Part of this you will already have done by thinking about your own nature (by considering archetypal powers) and by observing the way your own body operates (as in the use of asana).

The natural world and to a lesser degree, man made environments, can, if looked at correctly, provide you with just as much insight into the nature of self as the most 'head centred' exercises. Remember that, no matter how complex its' symbolism, your own deck is still a physical thing.

One of the major features of the micro/macrocosmic relationship is the two -way transmission of energy which is referred to as 'the tides'. The simplest examples of this are to be found in the cycle of the moon and the menstrual flux in women.

The movement of the moon sets the tides of the ocean to flow, certain sea creatures to breed and the level of Water to rise into the fruiting bodies of plants. The menstrual cycle in women causes an increase in introspection, sensitivity and psychic perception.

Both these cycles affect the consciousness of the female - one through the macrocosm and one through the microcosm. (Incidentally men also have a 'menstrual' or 'testiculatory' cycle although the physiological alterations in the case of a man are less obvious.) In most people their conscious mind attempts to override these tides, or totally ignore them. Our 'advanced' culture is only just becoming aware of the importance of inner and outer cycles, such as biorythms and sun-spot activity, and its' affect on humanity. Become aware of, and in doing so learn to work in harmony with the tides in the universe. Self development or exploration is not about the outward thrust of the self seeking out a place in reality and dissecting the forces which make it tick - it is about 'coming home' and re-connecting with the essential you.

Each card within your deck may be seen as an archetype but it must be stressed that ANY archetype has no meaning except in relation to others. No archetype can be exactly defined; they exist as psychological personifications of the titanic forces that create stars in distant space, and spin the D.N.A helix in every living cell. To begin with use the idea of the archetypal forces which you have already come across. Take four separate walks, three in 'natural locations' and one in a man-made locality. Don't try to find dramatic locations full of waterfalls and mountains. The only proviso is that the first three walks should be in places as free from the destructive impact of human beings as possible. The last walk should take you through a city, try to incorporate both the 'Brave New World' and 'wasteland' aspects of a city - perhaps from a new 'space-age' shopping mall to the older, forgotten backstreets and 'building sites'.

Give yourself at least half an hour before each walk (if you need to drive to the starting point of your journey give yourself a few moments before you start walking). In this time, relax your bodymind and allow thoughts to come and go as they will. Don't let your mind dwell on the forthcoming walk as this will provide you with an opportunity to develop preconceptions about the experience. Just relax and drift; in this way the journey will have an 'other-worldly' quality to it, almost like a dream. The aim is just to walk, not necessarily to get somewhere, and certainly not in any specific time.

Having this opportunity to relax, begin your walk, consider that you are going on a pilgrimage like The Fool in the tarot. Your 'pilgrimage' is not to any point, rather your whole journey is one to be made through a 'sacred space', i.e your environment. As you walk, become aware of the archetypal forces around you, thus if you see gulls in a refuse site you may understand them not as 'just gulls eating' but as an expression of the 'Scorpionic Archetypes' of dissipation, putrification and resurrection, or you might see a tree as the 'Mediator Archetype', linking both Earth and sky as in Atu I 'The Magus'.

As you walk let all your senses overtake you, smell the air. feel the buildings, listen to the sounds, in short rejoice in your environment. After your walk has ended you can switch on the analytical facilities of the mind again and record your results, however don't try to dissect them too far, for some things, like rabbits or Shakespeare's' plays will not yield more but will only die when subjected to over-zealous analysis.

Exercises

Absorption and Elimination.
Western society has divorced us from the essential importance of feeding, breathing and eliminating waste. In learning to understand the earth element it is useful to consider these simple body processes. The human body is as much a part of the whole of inner/outer nature as any other system and should never be overlooked (as is so often the case in modern re-interpretations of Indian and Oriental mysticism).

Begin by considering your food - not just as something to be crammed in between appointments, but as the essential fuel which animates your self.

Try the following:
Obtain a simple food item such as an apple or nuts. Fruit gathered from source, such as wild berries or from an 'organic' orchard is best. Spend a little time considering the food you are about to consume. Consider that the food you intend to eat has been forged through millions of years of evolution, become aware of the colour, smell, touch, then taste and sound of the food as it is eaten. Really think about what you are eating, almost as though it were a sacramental substance (which, of course, it is). Buy or collect some seeds which you can grow as a food plant. Don't just limit yourself to the 'traditional' vegetables; you could try sorrel, rosemary herb, even nettles or dandelions which make excellent salad vegetables. Plant them, tend them, and eat them. Try to see this activity not just as horticulture but as an way of connecting you to the earth which is your foundation. Experiment with new foods and drinks, see if you can find a natural spring in your location, become aware of your food as a living thing.

Investigate different qualities in the air. Consider air is also a food and comes in various forms. For example the smell and quality of the air differs in the morning, when the plant community begins to produce large volumes of oxygen. The feel of the air differs depending on the proportion of charged ions; thus prior to an electrical storm the air 'feels heavy', whereas in a cave or by a waterfall negatively charged particles in the air make it feel fresh and light.

Elimination from the body of undigested food and liquid is a vital part of its' total function. Again in Western society these processes are looked on as being unsavoury or even anti-social.

The material you expel from your gut is food for other creatures from insects to micro-organisms to plant forms. When you excrete you are linked directly to the ecology of the planet just as much as when you eat. Consider the fact, when next you visit the toilet, that you are ridding unwanted material from your body but are directly providing food for other creatures (although 'modern' sewerage systems have broken much of this cycle into disharmony). Investigate how the act of elimination may be used as a tool for relaxation and even inspiration (may people say that they often get their best ideas whilst sitting on the toilet. This is because they are probably alone, and able to relax their bodymind as their sphinctal muscles release). Imagine that when you rid your body of waste you are getting rid of all unbalanced, worn out energies and making room for new input both physically and psychologically.

Observation Techniques

Try the following:

1) Spend a week observing things in negative. (This technique is taught to art students and forms the basis of the Japanese art of flower arranging where it is not the flowers but the 'ma' or space that is arranged between them). See the leafless tree not as a series of lines through space but rather as a series of spaces between lines.

2) Spend at least one day just wandering around the centre of your home town. Observe the people who throng the streets, their dress, their gestures, their way of walking - remember they can all provide valuable insight. You are not necessarily very different to any of them.

3) Try to observe your environment selectively. Choose a category, such as 'things that are red' and at any time stop and look around, focusing your attention on just these elements of your environment. Move on later to categories which are less specific such as 'things I dislike' or 'things I

need to live'.

4) Watch shadows. Most people when they are asked 'what colour is a shadow' will answer 'black', your observation will show this to be untrue. Observe shadows formed by natural light, by streetlamps and house lighting. Watch the way shadows move across the plane on which they are cast and the way they change, particularly those cast by the sun, at different times of the day and year, and under different weather conditions.

5) See the way that the whole world of human and non-human interaction is mirrored in the tarot deck. Pick three cards, dividing the deck, if necessary, to make sure the third card is a Major Arcana one. Study the symbolism of the card and spend a week becoming aware of the reflections and different levels of this card present in your environment. (Thus should you choose Atu VI 'The Lovers' - you could see it manifest as two lovers walking down the street arm in arm, or the union of rain and sun which forms a rainbow).

Considering the Body

Take some time to become aware of the various esoteric views of the body and the healing process (see the booklist at the back of the book to help you with finding useful texts).

Experiment with yoga, massage techniques, and other systems which focus on the physical body. The following exercises will concentrate very much on your inner mindscape and it is vital to be firmly rooted in the physical reality of the body before you try them.

The Bioregion

The concept of the bioregion is as old as humanity, indeed as old as territorial lifeforms as a whole. Just as you must see your relationship to immediate nature (through your five senses) and personal nature (by studying your food, breath and elimination) so you should begin to understand your place in your immediate geographical surroundings. The concept of a bioregion is of an area in which an individual or group dwell which is marked by natural features as their immediate 'field of operations'. Examples of the bioregional concept are to be found in the fast vanishing tribal civilisations of Africa, South America and other lands. Communities define their place not by imagined boundaries on a map but by rivers, mountains, ancient trees, differences in altitude and

59

respective vegetation. In the urbanised landscape of Western society many of our natural reference points have been overwhelmed, yet there are still, even in cities, 'places of power'. However, you choose to view this power , get to know your own 'patch".

Obtain a set of maps and look out the bioregional features; areas of high ground, natural pools, old woodlands - and investigate them. Various symbols are associated with the cardinal points of the compass. These are one manifestation of the elemental four-fold division. 'Traditionally' the four elements are ascribed to the directions thus:

Direction	Element	Colours	
North	Earth	Green/Brown	Black
East	Air	Yellow	White
South	Fire	Red	Red
West	Water	Blue	Grey

This chain of correspondences is derived from bioregional features. The first series of colours given are those commonly used in modern magick, the second set are the colours ascribed the 'powers' of each direction by the British Celts. If you live in Britain then the elemental attribution of these directions will, if you consider and experience your natural environment become apparent. This system holds true for most areas around the Mediterannean also. If you live in another land other factors will apply. You may find that by exploring the features peculiar to your bioregion that you will discover a) just what you have always overlooked in the past b) places where you can go to rest, to meditate and just to enjoy their particular ambiance, and c) areas which you may wish to use later for ritual.

Finding Your Spot

In Carlos Castanadas' stories about Don Juan he talks about the techniques of finding your own 'spot' or place of power. This can be seen as an example of 'relational body language', that is body language which communicates information by the relationship between your own body and your environment. Examples of this are to be found in the phraseology of our own language, we talk of 'being the centre of attention', or 'sitting on the edge of your seat'. Most of us find our own 'places of power', perhaps a favourite chair or place in a room. Try experimenting with various 'spots' in the following ways.

Go to your quiet room or another location where you have a fair amount of space which is free from major distractions (you may wish to try this in some of the 'powerful places' you discovered in your own bioregion).

Mark out a circle at least six feet in diameter. This can be done with chalk, with a stick on the earth or with a length of twine. Slowly walk around the perimeter of the circle then move inward. Relax and breathe easily, then look for a place to sit. You may wish to sit on the perimeter or within the circle. It may take some time and trial and error to find a place in which you feel comfortable. Once you have done so, take a few moments to relax and appreciate your surroundings. Get used to your position in the context of the circle - this is especially important if you are outside (where factors such as shade and wind must be considered). Later, you may wish to ascertain which direction you are facing using a compass.

Record just where you sat and analyse your results. Were you sitting facing, or at, a cardinal point? Did you face inward to the centre of the circle or outward? Why do you think you did this?

In your quiet room array your cards around you, at random, starting to your right (where, in the Northern Hemisphere the sun rises) and work clockwise so that you finish in the 'East' and end up sitting in the centre of the circle. Does the fall of the cards follow any pattern? Is there a relationship between what you see in the fall of the cards and your choice of 'spot' in the above exercise.

Repeat this exercise by selectively placing the cards to mirror the features of your own bioregion. Thus if you have mountains or hills to the north-east of your home you could place 'earthy cards' such as the Queen of Disks in this region. As you begin to know your bioregion better you may wish to use more complex layouts to form a map of the forces in your locality. Begin by using just a few cards (say eight, four for the features of each cardinal point and four for the intercardinal directions).

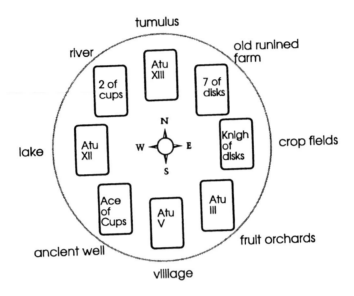

Earth Meditations

Sit in a comfortable asana in your quiet room. Relax and slow your breathing to a regular level. Let thoughts pass in and out of your mind as they will. When you are sufficiently relaxed imagine yourself going on a walk to one of the 'places of power' in your own bioregion. Try to recall the sights, smells, sounds and all the sensations you experienced.

This internal 'pilgrimage' exercise will probably be very difficult; you will have to hold, clearly, a complex group of imagined sensations. Choose a short walk and make an effort to keep your attention focused on this inner journey. On your travels around your own bioregion keep your eyes open for an object to use in this meditation. The object should be small enough to hold easily in your hands such as a stone, a pebble from the beach or a twig and should not have been arrived at by destruction of your own bioregion (incidentally it is often forgotten by 'new agers' that the 'sacred earth crystals' they croon over have been mined from areas such as South America which are already threatened with decimation by numerous other industries).

Go to your quiet room. Relax and hold you object it in your hands.

Reach out your mind and become conscious of its feel; that is both its physical texture (and if your eyes are open, appearance) and its own 'inner nature'. Even the meanest stone by the motorway has endured for thousands of years and thus has much to offer if you can learn to 'listen' to it in the correct way.

Reading for Others

Why read for others? The answers to this question vary widely from person to person. Some see divination by tarot as a manifestation of a 'gift' which they must use to assist others. Many people are simply drawn, often by circumstance, into such work. Whatever your motivation, even if it is unclear at present, you should certainly consider the nature of the tarot as a means of communication. In the context of reading for others there should be a two-way interchange of energy; you must learn from the experience of performing the reading just as your client is assisted by it (much as a good teacher will learn from their students). The energies described by each card should by now be familiar and, as you read, should draw you into their patterns. By completing the previous evaluation exercises, and by cultivating both objective logic and intuitional insight you will gain the knowledge and confidence to begin reading for others.

If you have been lucky enough to have had friends to volunteer as practice subjects, then you may have already begun to understand the interchanges of energy which occur when reading the cards for other people. As with any aspect of the tarots' use you will need to use information gained at all possible levels - logic, intuition and 'common sense', to decide whether or not to read in individual cases. There are certain guidelines which exist (not as dogmatic doctrine but rather as a 'code of conduct' evolved by the experience of many readers) to help you to decide for whom you should read, when, where and how.

The circumstances you will be asked to read under will vary; some querants are motivated by curiosity, some have immediate questions and other more long term problems. You will be asked everything, from picking the Derby winner to whether a man should seek a divorce from his wife. Your role as a tarot reader is a complex and vital one; you will be placed in the position, by your clients, of Priest-confessor, counsellor, teacher and vizor. You must undertake to be bound by the rules of confidentiality.

To allow the client to really 'open up' to you your oath of silence should be inviolate. The only exceptions to this rule would be where, in the course of your reading, you became aware that to withhold an item of information from a third party could result in loss of life or a violation of a fundamental human right. A querant may well divulge, within 30 minutes, a secret they have held alone for as many years. Your ability to gain access to information, unlimited by time, will often inspire the client to pour out their problems and childhood memories. It is often the case that you will touch such a problem using the cards, usually 'in abstract'. The client may then let the information come tumbling out - and it is often that the 'key' accessed via the tarot is the most important factor.

For the client to feel ready to talk about a long dormant fear is a mark of success, for the tarot is frequently a method of personal counselling where divining the future is of secondary importance. In reading you will asked to face a wide range of emotion and experiences; guilt, birth, death, love, anger, hopelessness and joy, and be asked to assist in the most complicated and tragic problems. Reading should not be treated as a game and you should not begin to advise others until you have gained a basic grasp of human nature, and therefore your own nature. It is as exacting and often painful for the reader as for the client. (These skills may be gained by a combination reading at an 'experimental' level, observation of human beings in the flesh, and study of basic psychological theory (see the reading list for texts which deal with this information)).

Before beginning your foray into reading for others it is advisable to initially know when not to read. The time and place are the initial factors. The time must be convenient for you - dealing with the hopes and fears of the world immediately after a hard day at the office is best avoided. Never be cajoled into doing a reading. As a reader you must direct the proceedings and be in control. Make appointments to fit in with your life; reading can be difficult enough without exhausting yourself by pandering to all comers, at any time. The time and place is determined by where and when you feel most comfortable, your own domain is often best, where you are 'strongest' and most relaxed. Unless absolutely necessary do not be tempted to read for two (or more) people simultaneously. Your intuitional focus may become confused and distorted as you attempt to follow two, perhaps divergent, threads of syncronicity. Even with close partners, one querant may be restrained from saying what they really want to say (this rule also avoids the problem of, for example, reading for a husband & wife and intuiting that one partner has a difficulty within the relationship and wishes to clarify that with you before talking to their partner).

It would also be ill-advised to read for a person who is seriously distressed or psychologically disturbed, as they may well misunderstand the information you give them and will probably not be able to assimilate and act on it in a constructive manner. (You may or course opt to postpone the reading until a time when the client is less fraught.) As a last point you should avoid the temptation to play the allseeing oracle. You will not be able to answer every question posed Allow for your limitations as well as your newly flourishing abilities.

One rule that should be adhered to if you decide to read for others, particularly on a 'professional basis', is that you should not tell a client that that they will die within such-and-such a time period, or in a certain way. Apart from the obvious moral implications you could find yourself in serious trouble (a smart lawyer could argue successfully that you had attempted to 'psychologically intimidate' their client). If you do see danger threatening try to establish its nature by intuition and careful questioning of your client. You may then wish to advise them, tactfully, to take a medical examination, or to make sure their car is serviced. In the rare situations where death is seen you should allow for the clients free will and should on no account share such information with your client.

So how should you begin? You will want to set the stage. Arrange seating, levels of light etc.. to provide a comfortable and relaxing atmosphere. Candlelight and the use of a special cloth on which to lay the cards will help to focus both your mind, and that of your client on the work in hand. You may wish to burn a light incense whilst reading, the aim is to focus your mind on the impressions gained via the tarot - a prodigious amount of esoteric paraphernalia will tend to lead you away from your focus. Having composed yourself and made your client welcome, invite them to sit down and begin by talking to them about general matters, perhaps making them a cup of tea. Allow them to 'unwind'.

At this point, and indeed throughout the reading, you should make an effort to be aware of their body language. Are their arms and legs folded ? Are they sitting back from you or leaning intently forward? Use this information to help you to ascertain their state of mind. Explain briefly how the tarot works and what you are going to do, establish if your client has had a reading before and how that reading was conducted.

Establish with your client that reading is not a guessing game. The odd sceptic will arrive, asking you to prove what you can do; you should not feel bound to prove anything, those with totally closed minds will never accept even the most lucid demonstration of divination nor should you debase your abilities to perform parlour tricks for the mildly curious. But be wary before refusing a person with such an attitude, as they may be using a mask of hardened rationalism to cover a fear that the Tarot really works. Tell your client what feedback you require. It is possible to read for a client who gives no response whatsoever, although this is far from the ideal. You must have confidence in the validity of your impressions to be able to cope with such a situation, it is often that a 'silent type' feels that, or has been told previously, that a reader should not be interrupted. Alternatively you may have a client who insists on talking throughout the reading. It is essential to have command of the reading - tell your client when you would like a response. Get such information from your client as will allow you, to avoid the 'guessing game' situation; for example you may see healing, violence and death in the cards and become somewhat confused, yet by ascertaining that your client is a nurse in an accident & emergency department, you need not waste twenty minutes of the reading. There is little point in imparting contemporary knowledge that your client already has, for this serves only to bolster your own ego and provide some form of 'confirmation' to the sceptic - neither of which is very useful. Most importantly say what you see, if you see pink elephants, or get the impression that your client is going to visit Antarctica say so, there is no use in missing vital information simply because you feel embarrassed or wary of making a mistake. You can be wrong or make a slight error and not need to abandon the reading or put your cards into moth-balls. Go back on your intuition and re-interpret your impressions, gain new information from your client, to assist in developing a context for your thoughts. Don't be afraid to make and acknowledge, your mistakes - learn from them.

It is perfectly acceptable to use methods other than just your intuitional powers to determine the nature of the clients' problems, or present state. As previously mentioned, body language, observation of dress, speech and mannerism all play an important part in developing a human context in which to fit the information gained intuitively. Lay the foundation of your reading with a broad study of your client, but don't be fooled into judging a book by its' cover.

There are methods of using information offered by the client in a rather limited way. One method of this is the rather insultingly named 'Gypsy Trick'. With this practice a skillful but charlataneous reader draws information from client, restates the same information, and returns it to the client who becomes convinced that the reader has a remarkable insight into themself. (Such readings often start "..ah I see that when you were a child you had a favourite toy..." - the client is immediately startled by such an amazing insight. The 'reader' them implants a series of suggestions "... and you took your favourite toy to bed with you" - the client then begins to slip deeper into the scenario created. "...and you felt lonely so you cuddled your favourite toy..." etc.. It is easy to be taken in by one skilled in this practice - (politicians do it all the time.) Don't be afraid to say what you see and don't limit your perception of the client simply by their outward appearance; even if the querent is ninety-four she could be about to get married, the person with holes in their jeans may not be poor but rather a rock star.

This leads us to the question of various moral issues with regard to divination for others - the first being the importance of cultivating an objective and non-judgmental attitude. You have your own belief structure - be it Buddhist, Hindu, Wiccan or whatever but you should not impose any of your own ethical or philosophical ethos on your client. You cannot afford to limit your intuition nor can you make judgements on your clients' actions. Your role is to listen and to act as vizor but not as moral teacher or guru. However, if you are asked something which you cannot answer because of a deep personal conviction (for instance if a racist asks you how they can best evict the black family living in the flat above them) then you may elect to terminate the reading.

With regard to religious belief, you should become acquainted with your clients own world- view; for instance if you are a Wiccan you may suggest that your client should seek out the Goddess force, but if your client is a Catholic you could express this by suggesting that they burn a candle to the Virgin Mary. This point is vital - for the tarot to be a useful means of communication you must be able to garb your intuition in a series of symbols or ideas to which your client can relate. Use words your client is familiar with, and point out that if at any time your client is unsure about what you mean then they should ask you to explain. If you are speaking to a business man try to use ideas which they will identify with, if your client is a musician or mechanic then another facet of language may be required.

Take a detached but interested approach to what you are told or intuite for the client - try not to be shocked or upset. This leads us to the question of dealing with emotional difficulties. Maintaining a totally unsympathetic approach would be useless to you both; but to allow yourself and your client to dissolve into tears may be a relief but may not necessarily be very productive. If your client needs to cry give them 'space' and tissues but keep talking calmly.

This brings us to the the ethics of taking money for divination consultations. A tarot reading must be a two way procedure. 'Traditionally' there was always an exchange for the reading, the traditional 'silver sixpence' for instance. In any case, you will have to consider your own relationship to those you read for in terms of whether or not to charge, and if so how much. Money is the dominant cultural system of exchange in the Western world, but there is nothing to stop you asking to be paid 'in kind' perhaps you could ask your client to bring a loaf of bread and jar of coffee, or, particularly in the case of those who need a reading but are unable to pay, a service offered (such as baby-sitting).

So just what is being paid for? One way of looking at it is this; your skill as a reader is free, but your tea, electricity, house etc, is not. The client pays for your time, not necessarily for your abilities. You cannot afford to keep working for free and thereby neglecting yourself - the best divinatory skills are useless if they make you a slave to the needs of others and render you unable to help yourself. You can only really help others if you can keep your own house in order first. If money is exchanged you may wish to calculate this on a sessional basis as a reading could last anything from 40 minutes to two hours.

The last factor is closing the reading: be sure of yourself, when you judge the time is right put the cards away. Don't be tempted to continue for hours prompted by a client who wants more than you can give. Give yourself time and don't rush the process, remember each session could hold a multiplicity of possibilities and you cannot really know just how simple or deep the reading will be until you begin. There generally comes a point at which one 'thread of synchronicity' has been followed as far as you are able for the moment, stop then, perhaps suggesting, if necessary, that the client returns some time later to let you know how things have worked out, or for another reading.

Exercise

Try doing some readings!

- # Communication & Communion

The following exercises are designed to allow you to examine the relationship between yourself and other human beings. Self development means actively accepting change, and you will find that your relationships with other people may change. This could put a strain on your relationships with your partner, children, parent or boss. This is not because you are becoming a more exulted being but simply because you will be evaluating and analysing your relationships more deeply than before.

Exercises

Explaining the Unexplainable

By now you will almost certainly have been asked to explain just what you are 'getting into'. If this has occurred, analyse the way you explained the tarot. Consider the way you explain even the simplest of things, such as directions to assist a traveller, or teaching a child to tie shoelaces.

Construct a flow chart to show the order in which you would explain the most important points of any given aspect of your studies. What information would you need to establish from the querent? How would you explain the apparent complexity of magickal terminology?

The Alien Game

This game is one that must be played with at least one other person. One person elects to play the alien. The alien has a humanoid form and must be consistent in what they do and do not understand of human culture, and also in what they say about their home planet. The alien will also understand human language but not necessarily the exact meaning of certain terms e.g 'family', 'male & female' or social concepts such as 'class', 'nations' and 'discipline'.

The alien then initiates a conversation, perhaps prompted by looking an an object such as a cigarette and says something like 'I'm an alien, just landed on your world. What is this?'

The other people then explain to the alien about the object, its uses and meaning. This game can be hilarious and provides an excellent opportunity to see just how you define, and therefore comprehend, concepts from sexuality to organic gardening.

Newspaper View
Take several different newspapers on one day and compare the reporting of a single event. How do they differ and on what points do they agree? Why do you think such differences of view occur?

Radio Days
Listen to a radio programme, where you cannot receive any information in the form of body language or eye contact. How do you obtain your information about what is being said, other than by the words used (i.e the intonation of speech, pauses between words and the use of emotive phrases)? Listen to radio drama and see how a skilled performer can express an emotion by sound, allowing you to create a mental picture of the character being portrayed.

Television
Turn on the television with the sound down, observe the actions of people, particularly in chat shows and debates. Watch the body language and actions of those involved in the programme. Watch how people demonstrate their relationship to others by gesture, eye contact and movement. How can you tell if someone interviewed is nervous, angry or enthusiastic ? How often do the visual clues contradict the body language? (skilled politicians, when angry often sit and smile coolly).

Character Communication
When reading a novel, notice how the author gives away clues in the text to allow you to draw a composite picture of a characters' nature. Observe how, by being given a character sketch in the book you will often know, ahead of the narrative itself, how the character will react in a given situation.

Cultural Exchange
Watch Asian Temple Dancing, modern balletic or oriental dance forms where each ritual gesture communicates information to the audience. Even if you do not know the complexity of 'dance' language, can you ascertain the meaning of some of the gestures displayed? Listen to classical music, such as Grieg's 'Peer Gynt' or 'Peter & The Wolf' where the sounds of

certain instruments are used to represent a particular scene or character.

Childs' Play
Watch young children and the way they communicate. See how an older brother or sister will act as interpreter for a baby or the way that children with different spoken languages will play together and evolve, very rapidly, their own linguistic means of communication.

Different Molds
Watch or imagine people in different contexts. For example the Ronald Reagan in the B Movie 'Bedtime for Bonzo' is a very different man from Ronald Reagan President of the U.S.A. (or is he?). Notice how dress affects the way people feel, behave and are viewed by others - the business man in his suit (of armour), the bricklayer dressed as a barmaid for a fancy dress party, the doctor in his long white coat. Consider the idea of uniforms. What purpose does this serve?

Investigating Thought
Examine and learn a little about various religious, ethical and philosophical systems from Catholic Christianity to modern Paganism. How does each belief system change the way that its' adherents act and think? Observe how people with different beliefs can have a totally different perspective on the same object, event or issue (remember the newspaper exercise).

All the exercises given above illustrate that the behaviour and personality traits you see in other people are also within you. By looking at others, their faults, strengths, methods of thought and action you can begin to recognise these characteristics in yourself. Record all your results and relate them to yourself.

Communication, Communion & Community
Make a positive effort to contact other people with whom you can communicate about subjects such as the tarot. Contact others through notices in occult shops or contact magazines. Don't go out looking for a guru skilled in the tarot or any sort of 'spiritual partner' or 'companion on the path'. Take the opportunity to meet, speak to and share information with another like-minded person.

Mediation

Monitor your thoughts and speech. Every time you find yourself using pessimistic or limiting phraseology stop yourself and be silent for a moment. Begin again, using more positive and expansive words without fooling yourself into looking at the world through a rose tinted brain.

Seize the opportunity to talk to people - in the bus queue, or at work. Most people will gladly talk, on a long, boring bus ride, once they realise you just want to chat. Find something innocuous to begin the conversation, such as the state of the weather. You may be surprised by who you meet and just how interesting that dull bus ride can become.

- **The Flow of Magick**

Water moves, ebbs, flows and connects. In the physical world the element of water covers two thirds of the globe, moved by the gravitational forces of the sun and moon. In living things, water is continuously exchanged both within individual cells and tissues and between plants, animals and bacteria.

In magick, the element of water represents forces which interconnect, or flow through, all levels of reality. Water represents emotionality, and the energy interchanges by which sensitivity can be perceived by the self. In magick the term 'energy' is often used to describe invisible forces; this may apply to emotions (emotions themselves cannot be seen, only the behaviour resulting is perceptible

A large proportion of self-development involves the development of sensitivity to these 'invisible energies', then how to direct, accept and integrate them within the self. Magick is not about learning to impose your will over the natural order of the universe; the lesson of the water element is that strength comes from being able to flow with the currents in the cosmos, not against them.

Bodies of Water

Having explored your own bioregion you will have probably encountered numerous sources and forms of water. Begin this exercise by considering water in its' physical form, remembering that the nature of the elements is such that the characteristics they display at one level are repeated on others.

Investigate various bodies of water in your own bioregion, waterfalls, pools, lakes, streams, perhaps even the ocean. Touch, swim and investigate the water in your area. Become aware of the 'moods' of water in rain, mists, calm waters, thundering waves etc..

Be aware of the other manifestations of water; within your food, as the sap in plants, and the blood circulating within your body.

The water element represents feeling, in the truest sense of the word. In magickal parlance, water symbolises intuition and is characterised as being the ruling element of the 'astral plane': the level of impressions, emotions and dreams. It is the astral level which magickal theory describes as being the well-spring (another watery analogy) of imagination. Like water, astral reality is reflective and malleable (i.e easily influenced; just as still water can be whipped into dramatic waves by a gentle wind).

In the use of the tarot, the astral or water aspect is related to divination. From a self exploratory perspective this level will require you to draw on your experience of organised imagination to 'feel' the forces depicted in the cards. The elements qualities within you must be allowed to work equally and in harmony if they are to find unity in the matrix termed Spirit.

The watery element is notoriously difficult, for water is the element of illusion. Part of the rationale behind the physical, earthly exercises of bodymind discipline are that they will help you to avoid what magickians call confusing the planes. Basically, this means getting so wrapped up in the astral dream world that it becomes mistaken for the sum total of reality rather than just a part. Western industrialised society has trampled down the imaginative functions of the self to such an extent that, in learning to accept 'fantasy' as having a valid place in your total reality, you may experience a sort of 'kick back' effect. Attention to your magickal record and to the 'mundane' part of living will provide you with an anchorage so that you explore the watery aspects of being without drowning in the waters of unqualified fancy.

Exploring your own Energies

Begin by becoming aware of the subtle energies which animate your Self.

Go to your quiet room and try the following exercises:

1) Holding your hands about six centimetres apart, feel the energy which flows between them. Imagine the energy between your palms as a ball of light (if you are a visually orientated person you may wish to see it as being composed of light or blue light). Play with this ball of energy; move your hands around this globe of energy, make it grow, change its' colour - just see what you can feel.

2) Energy in music. Choose some appropriate music to listen to, don't

just listen to the sound but feel it - what emotions, pictures or other sensations does the music bring to mind. Use a relaxing 'watery' recording (be wary in using 'new age' type 'muzak' as it tends to superficiality and does not allow sufficient scope for exploration) - music that you may find suitable for this is suggested at the back of this book.

3) Feeling Words. Relax your bodymind and begin to repeat a single word or phrase, slowly. You may wish to select a tarot card at random and repeat its' title. Begin by saying the word aloud and after about ten minutes, silently. The repetition of the word will automatically regulate your breathing and the sound is not so much said as felt - the word flows through you. This should help you experience how energy flows.

Psychometry

Psychometry is the ability to gain impressions or information relating to the past, present or future of an object, by touching it. People who are skilled in psychometry are able to take an item of personal jewellery and obtain impressions from it about the wearer, important situations and possible events in their life. The technique used is to hold or place your hands on the object and allow your awareness to open up. You may wish to imagine your awareness opening out like a lotus blossom until you begin to feel impressions. Try psychometrising various objects; jewellery, standing stones, trees, old buildings. Don't aim your thoughts at any particular piece of information just see if you can feel anything from these objects other than the information that the limited use of your five senses provides.

Try the following exercises:

I) Shuffle the cards and lay the pack, face down, in front of you.

II) Draw one card from the deck (cutting the deck if you feel this is necessary).

III) Open out your awareness and see if you can name the card without looking at it.

IV) Record your choice and then place the card face down to one side of the pile.

When you have gone through the whole deck, check your results. You may wish to begin by ascertaining which suit a card is or if it is a Major Arcana card.

The Chakras & the Astral Body

One of the most commonly used methods of describing the energies which exist at various levels in the bodymind or micro/macrocosm, is through the chakra system. The term chakra is of Asian derivation and may be translated as 'wheel', 'sphere' or 'centre'. Just as the physical body may be mapped in terms of vital organs, nerves, bones, lymphatic system etc.., so the other, non-physical or 'subtle' levels of the body may be described using other maps. Various systems involving the chakra exist, some use five, nine thirteen or more 'file headings', but by far the most

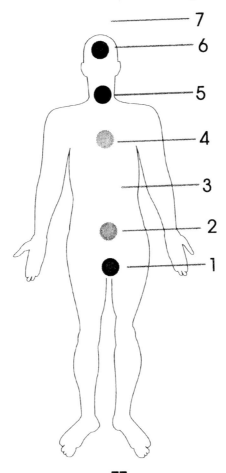

commonly used is the seven-fold system.

Each centre is interrelated (just like physical organs) and none is more important or 'spiritual' than any other. Each chakra governs various psycho-physical, emotional and metaphysical functions of the self. Each chakra may be imagined as a lotus which opens when a certain level of awareness is reached. The chakra system is opening in you, right now! However, conditioning may have repressed certain aspects of their function (or caused 'blocks' to form in the subtle energy flow), and you may not be aware of their function - this is magick raising the awareness of the individual to comprehend the essential simplicity of that which was previously imagined as complex, unknowable or illusionary.

1. Base chakra. Situated at the base of the spine. Symbolic colour; red. Regulates the basic sexual desires (i.e lust in the truest sense of the word, as expressed in Atu XI 'Lust').

2. Navel chakra, situated about two inches below the navel. Symbolic colour; orange. This centre is akin to the 'centre' of martial arts. It links the 'root forces' of the first centre to the inner and outer universes of the self.

3. Solar Plexus Chakra, situated in the area of the solar plexus. Symbolic colour: yellow. Emotions, intuition and transmission of subtle energy (from one level to another) are governed by this centre.

4. Heart Chakra, situated in the centre of the torso in the region of the heart. Symbolic colour; green. This centre governs desire in the sense of love - in the sense of compassion and desire for communion with other people, levels of reality or entities.

5. Throat chakra, situated at the base of the throat. Symbolic Colour: blue. This is the place of the word, i.e the conceptualising and expressing of self to others.

6. Third Eye chakra, situated about one inch above the bridge of the nose. Symbolic colour; indigo. Psychic perception and 'thinking' are governed by this region; it is the seat of consciousness (in either its' unexpanded or limited form).

7. Crown chakra, situated about one inch above the top of the head. Symbolic colour; violet. Self illumination, timelessness, formlessness and totality are regulated by the function of this region.

There are many different ways of looking at the chakra system. If you have not already done so, read the books dealing with this subject detailed in the booklist, prior to, or following the exercises below.

1. Go to your quiet room (or try this outside where you will not be disturbed). Sit or stand in a comfortable position. Relax your bodymind and allow your hands to hang by your sides. Focus your attention on your base chakra, visualise, or feel it. Breathe in (through your nose) and as you do so raise your hands upward either side of you. When your lungs are full your arms should be held out to form a 'V' shape. Exhale and lower your hands. As you do this feel the breath energising and awakening the base chakra. If you are visualising, imagine it glowing a brighter, clear and incandescent red.

Repeat this process for each chakra. Repeat the process once more and become aware of your breath vitalising all the chakras simultaneously. Relax and return to 'normal' consciousness.

(You may find that, after practice, you will be able to feel all the chakras clearly. Problems with one or more, often indicate that you have some form of 'blockage' occurring at that level. A man who finds it difficult to speak his mind could find difficulty in imagining and vitalising his throat chakra. You may also find that, spontaneously when imagining the crown chakra it, all the centres 'turn white'. This occurs when all the energies are harmonised. Each is a colour in the visual spectrum which, when united in equality, becomes white light.)

2. Select seven cards from your deck which you think/feel represent most closely the seven chakras.

Place them in front of you in a line with the base chakra nearest to you and the crown chakra furthest away.

Relax your bodymind and slow your breathing. Focus your attention on the base card. As you breathe in and out, imagine a ray of white light touching upon the first (base) card and flowing towards the next. Repeat the breath cycle, focusing your attention on the second card, imagine it being illuminated by the white light which then flows on towards the next card. Repeat this practice until each card is bathed in the flow of white light. Breathe out and imagine the white light being absorbed into your body (you could imagine each card sending a ray of light into the corresponding chakra in your body). Relax.

3. Take the time to consider your chakras and to use them in your daily life. For instance if you are involved in playing football before the game, focus your attention on your base and navel chakra (the base for strength and drive and navel for manifestation of that drive in a team sense). If you need to speak with clarity and force, such as during a lecture, focus your attention on your throat chakra and feel it become invigorated and vibrant with power.

The Aura

The aura is a field of energy projected by the chakras and exists in an egg-shaped field of subtle power around the body (this is present in humans, animals, plants and even inanimate objects). According to certain theories the chakras create the aura which in turn form the body (at all levels). The term seeing the aura is in fact misleading as many people do not 'see' anything but feel the aura, much as one might talk about 'the aura of a room'. Even if you are not a visually orientated person (and are therefore more likely to 'feel' rather than 'see') you may still wish to describe your perceptions in terms of colour and/or elemental qualities.

The aura is divided into numerous layers (rather like an onion skin). The most commonly referred to are the etheric which usually exist one to three inches from the surface of the body and the 'outer' or astral aura which is egg shaped and of some nine feet in diameter (in a healthy individual). The most noticeable aura you see is the 'body area' or 'personal space' which we all have as a sort of immediate territory around us (the study of movement within this 'personal space' is the basis of body language).

Try a few simple experiments:

1. Observe the way both you and others move in your 'personal space' (this area is usually some six feet in diameter and again may be described as being egg shaped). At what distance do you feel, or do others feel, that

their personal space is threatened? Watch how women will accept children (even other peoples' children) into their space. Observe how people in a crowded train attempt to preserve this psychological territory.

2. As your awareness grows you may find yourself automatically becoming aware of the auric field. Try looking at people, animals, plants, your own limbs (or even whole body in a large mirror). The trick is not to look at but to focus past or beyond the subject, and to 'open-up' and sense. (You may also wish to focus your attention on your third eye chakra as this is the centre which governs 'second or psychic sight'.)

Beware of placing too much emphasis on anything you see/feel; remember that the mechanisms of the physical eye can play tricks on you, and that your perception, even of an actual aura, may be coloured by your prejudices or fancies. Phil Hine in his book 'Walking Between the Worlds' explains 'seeing the aura' thus, "There is an old story about a young man who read a book about auras of trees and their different colours. He spent a great deal of time trying to concentrate on seeing the auras of trees; alas, with little success. One day he considered a rowan tree, and wondered what the aura would look like, if only he could see it. He thought that it would be a kind of golden, russet-brown. with yellowish edges and...and suddenly he realised that he was seeing the tree's aura! He realised that seeing auras was not so much about seeing something physical, more a case of opening your mind to impressions. As sight is our dominant sense, we tend to interpret these impressions in terms of visual images such as colour, but there is no reason why we cannot use other senses as well. It's also worth remembering that very often, we see what we expect to see, not what is actually there."

3. Look through your tarot deck and make a note of all the chakra and aura representations and the images which appear therein.

Dreaming

Dreams occur when the consciousness moves from perceiving with the physical senses, to perceiving via the astral body. Once again dream reality comprises a number of levels; day dreams or periods of reverie, dreams which focus on the events of the day or week, recurrent dreams which are often related in our past to childhood events and dreams, the themes of which are much more deeply rooted in the unconscious. It is vital, particularly when dealing with water exercises, that you keep a record of your dreams. Each dream should be analysed; what precipitated the dream or the elements within the dream? How was the dreamscape molded? In most dreams, their symbolism, with a little thought, is quite obvious. If you have problems in analysing them, try to divide the elements within the dream into the properties of earth, water, air and fire. Select cards which seem to represent a figure from a dream and contemplate the card to find the key to the figures' meaning.

Remember that your boss or sister may appear in a dream but such a figure may be concealing a deeper meaning (even if that meaning is only that you should refrain from eating cheese before bed!) Dreams, like good books, contain many layers of meaning. If you are interested in further research look for an easy to read psychological text, don't bother consulting one of the numerous 'dream dictionaries' which are available, as they provide little more than guides to amusing parlour games.

One of the most interesting forms of dreaming is that known as 'lucid dreaming' or in esoteric terms astral travelling. Both these terms refer to the occasions where the subject is dreaming but is aware that they are doing so, or, more accurately, fully conscious on another level of reality.

The following techniques will, with perseverance, allow you to enter this state at will.

1. Before sleep, focus on your hands. Say to yourself 'I want to see my hands in my dream'. Upon dreaming you may well dream of your own hands and the resultant 'shock' will cause you to regain consciousness but remain within the dream or astral level. Then go exploring - another level of reality is open for business!

2. Set your alarm so that you will be woken at a predetermined time. To increase your dream recall, set the alarm to go off either about two hours after you fall asleep or around the time the sun rises (at these periods most people are firmly engaged in R.E.M., 'rapid eye movement' sleep - i.e dream sleep). By going through the motions, mentally, before

sleep, of turning off your alarm you may find that, just before the alarm sounds, you will enter a lucid dream.

3. The tatvic ('tattva' in the singular) symbols are a group of elemental images which are derived from Asian sources and may be used as doorways into the various areas in the astral level.

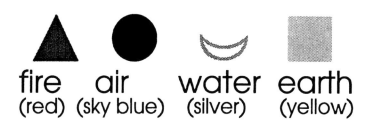

fire   air   water   earth
(red)   (sky blue) (silver)   (yellow)

Before you sleep visualise one of the tattvas. You may wish to draw or paint one of these symbols on a piece of card and keep it by your bedside or even affixed to the ceiling over your bed. Try to maintain the visualisation of the symbol for as long as possible before sleep intervenes. As you become more and more sleepy, imagine yourself moving toward the tattva, ready to step through it into the appropriate area of the astral.

Pathworking

Lucid dreaming requires you to be asleep, but in pathworking the individual relaxes the bodymind but does not at any point lose consciousness.

There are many variations of pathworking methods commonly employed in modern occulture. Systems such as the tarot, elemental symbolism, qabalah and many others are used to provide 'map references' to the mindscape of the individual. These 'map references' are based on archetypal units which are common to all people - thus the symbolism given through the mechanism of the Qabalah or the shamanic traditions of the North American Indians are, essentially, identical. Pathworking involves using a system of mapping the mindscape and plotting a route through the self. The sign posts are defined by the symbolic nature of the area accessed and woven in such a way as to provide an 'imaginative fantasy' which will lead the individuals' consciousness to arrive at a specific point in the astral realm.

The mechanism of pathworking follows a set pattern.

I) Definition. to begin with you must define the purpose of your pathworking. The purpose may be quite general, thus you might wish to do a pathworking using Atu XVIII 'The Moon' 'to explore the nature of the lunar force'. The force you are exploring is not something to be seen in isolation from yourself. By exploring 'The Moon' you are investigating the archetypal areas of you which are 'bound up' under the 'figure heading' of Atu XVIII. An effective pathworking will have long term consequences to both the micro and macrocosmic areas of your being. Through pathworking you can integrate the forces of your conscious and unconscious minds. You can analyse repressed features in your own mindscape and begin the process of getting to 'know thyself'. This process also has its analogue in the 'objective' universe; you may find your relationships, your physical circumstances and a plethora of other factors will also change as a result of even the most apparently simple pathworking.

II) Construction. If you are going to travel in the mindscape you must begin by plotting your route - sorting out the symbolic 'land marks', defining how your journey will begin, progress, reach a peak (destination) and conclude. The construction of pathworkings is a skilled business and requires you to have a firm grasp of human nature; which symbols produce which effects, how much detail to include, and how to instigate the beginning and termination of the pathworking in the most productive manner. Essentially, constructing an effective pathworking is like writing a play or novel - there must be just sufficient information to hold the attention and evoke a reaction from the audience, but not so much as to make the plot self-evident in the first few lines. The symbolism and procedures within your pathworking must be harmonious with the archetypal force you want to investigate. As well as using books on symbolism, psychology and the imagery given in your own card, you should also use your own experience, intuition and reason to determine what elements will play a part in the pathworking.

III) Delivery. This factor will often be decided by necessity rather than choice. The best method of pathworking is the 'story teller' method. This involves one person reading a carefully prepared script to the subject. The script is the pathworking and the listeners are the 'travellers'. The benefits of this method are obvious, especially if the reader is a person skilled in the use of these techniques. The reader can establish by breathing, posture and the aura, just what level of awareness the travellers are at and alter the script as necessary - e.g spend more time on the relaxation of the travellers, or speed up the pace of the pathworking if it is apparent that they are receptive. This method also allows an element of surprise to be introduced so that the travellers can allow the imagery free access from their unconscious minds and not start pre- empting what the reader is about to say. They will of course know that the purpose of the pathworking is to investigate the nature of Atu XVIII but the way the journey progresses will only be known in outline.

Taped readings for pathworking are useful but cannot be set to give the appropriate pauses in the journey that the individual may require (most of the 'new age' pathworking tapes have preliminary relaxation sections which are far too short for most people, and don't allow them to reach a sufficient level of quintessence before beginning the journey. They can also be confused by the use of monotonous 'muzak' which tends to hinder rather than help.)

If your pathworking explorations are to be conducted alone then you will have to use the 'chain of thought' method. This is akin to following a pre-scripted daydream, we will assume that this method is the one open to you, although the pathworkings given could be just as easily translated into a script for a reader or tape recorded by you and played back.

The stages, given below, outline the structure of most pathworkings. These stages form the skeleton of the pathworking which the flesh of specific imagery fills to create the whole body.

The Body; preparation of the bodymind complex should follow the pattern previously used in preparation for meditation.

Pathworkings should be conducted in your quiet room, again use incense sparingly. don't use music as this will only confuse the issue. Relax your bodymind, perhaps using the induction technique (or a variant) given at the end of this chapter or the method of focusing your sense of hearing on distant sounds and then drawing your awareness inward.

Temple: when your conscious mind is relaxed and centred then you have entered your own 'earth temple'. This is the 'home base' from which to begin your explorations.

Doorway: the doorway you select will depend upon the area of the mindscape you wish to explore. You could use one of the tattvic symbols, a tarot card, an imagined sound or a combination of visual and non-visual symbolism (e.g passing through a waterfall) the symbol should be such that you can imagine yourself stepping through it and entering a predetermined level in your unconscious.

Journey: upon entering the required mindscape, you will want to explore or at least observe your surroundings. You will need to begin your journey through the landscape, prompting your unconscious mind by suggesting the general features and ambiance of the mindscape (e.g - for a fire pathworking; 'the land is dark and black clouds hang low in the sky. Thorny trees and strange cacti dot the landscape, the air is warm and smells of burning wood and aromatic spices...etc.').

Ordeal: To gain full access it is often necessary to instigate a sort of trial within the fabric of the pathworking - thus mimicking the IAO formula (see chapter XXX). Again the way this manifests will depend on the nature of the journey in question. (E.g - for our fire pathworking; 'you see before you a curtain of flames, blazing as high as the sky and away into the distance. You know you must walk through the flames but know that they will not burn you - step through them...etc.).

Journey (with goal in sight): After the ordeal you will need to define a focal point on which you can have your sights set - the inner sanctum of the particular level you are exploring. (E.g - having passed through the curtain of flames you see before you a mountain top upon which stands a temple, and you know that it is the centre of the elemental plane of fire - your destination).

Destination: Having arrived at the core of your pathworking you will need to script a method, compatible with the nature of the pathworking, for you to commune with the 'innermost light' therein. (E.g 'the central chamber in the fire temple has three sides and is illuminated by a light on each wall, one is a bright burning flame, one a yellow globe of warm light and the third an arching electrical energy field. In the centre of the floor, standing tall and straight is a wand - the central generator of each of the three fiery energies that is around you.').

Gaining: Once firmly established in the core of the pathworking, you will need to go through a script that allows you to 'bring back' an element from that level. By doing so you will activate the forces encountered at a conscious level and will be able to integrate them. (E.g. 'you reach out, knowing that the wand standing before you is the essence of your own fiery nature. Take it, for it is given freely to you, to carry with you and to use wisely etc.').

Doorway: Having obtained the lesson from the core (perhaps, as in our example, symbolised by an object - i.e the wand), you can take a short cut via the same or a similar doorway that leads you into the pathworking scenario. (E.g 'turning around, you see that behind you a doorway, in the form of a red triangle has formed. Concentrate on the symbols, make the shape firm and well defined. Now step through it...').

Return: Immediately you have returned you will need to ease yourself back into the earth level. You may also input the suggestion in your mind that you will recall all that you have experienced (this should be affirmed from the obtaining section of the pathworking). (E.g. 'now you can feel again the air as it passes through your body, the ground beneath you, the sounds outside of this room. Awake, but remember all that you have seen, and heard, and smelt and touched and tasted and bring these things with you as you awake, alert, relaxed and comfortable - awake').

A Word of Warning

Pathworking methods, despite what some armchair psychologists may tell you, are not dangerous techniques. For most people the only real problem they encounter is the tendency to fall asleep during the induction stage. There are a few occasions where a pathworking may hit a 'soft spot' in your own psyche and an apparently minor exploration will open the flood gates of long repressed memories, thoughts and feelings. If this happens the key is to accept, analyse and synthesise. First be aware of what you feel - don't question it but let the emotion or memory play through you. Then begin to examine just what you are experiencing (more of this in the Air Chapter), use meditation and analysis to examine your feelings. Then begin to synthesise the feeling - perhaps by adapting and reworking your script you can complete the transformational process (again more of this in the Fire chapter). Major upsets are quite rare, particularly if you have done your ground work well and are provided with the earthly anchors of environmental understanding, people knowledge and self-discipline. After all, nobody said it was going to be easy!

Physically, eating and drinking following a pathworking is a good idea, to help 'ground' or centre your bodymind. You may find that your hands and feet feel a little cold, (this, according to magickal theory is because your astral and physical bodies have become temporarily less well connected to each other) A warm environment to perform the journey in and possibly a blanket over the feet may help. A warming drink afterwards will help to stabilise your body temperature. A commonly encountered problem is that you may not want to return to the earth plane. This problem is comparatively minor. An ideal pathworking will begin to instill the suggestion that the individual will awaken refreshed and alert towards its conclusion. (One of the best techniques if you are pathworking with others is to call the persons' name, or use a 'word of command'; e.g. 'wake up!'. If this does not have any immediate effect, pull the big toes of the individual who is reluctant to return to the physical level. The big toes are connected to a set of meridians - the lines of energy used in acupuncture - which, when pulled, release energy which encourages the realignment of the physical and astral bodies.)

In any case the issue of confusing the planes, should be remembered. The astral realm can be addictive, a sort of endless 'head-trip' escapism in which everything is sweetness, light and crystalline angelic entities. In terms of your record the tendency to become absorbed in the astral level may be combated by disciplined keeping of your results. As with dreams the experiences gained from each pathworking should be written down, in detail, as soon as possible. Later, you can analyse your experiences to learn more about yourself (as you are/were when the pathworking was done), and make plans for future exercises, inner journeys or subjects to explore.

A Note on Imagery

A pathworking must contain imagery and pauses suitable for allowing natural imagery to well up from the unconscious. For example in a pathworking concerned with the Ace of Cups you could 'see a chalice' - some people will see the chalice as being a silver goblet whereas other might see a gourd bowl or simple horn cup. The unconscious is free to generate whatever images are correct at the time rather than being bound to any particular description e.g 'you see a silver chalice with six blue jewels around the rim which is seven inches in diameter etc.'. By analysing the images the unconscious mind produces you will be able to determine the depth and specific area of the mindscape which the conscious mind has accessed (we will go into 'post pathworking analysis' in the next hexagram chapter).

With practice you will find that constructing pathworkings for yourself or others becomes increasingly easy. Although the journey will be, as our earthly life is, dominated by visual images you should aim for a 'total experience'. For instance, in the 'gaining' part of the pathworking script you could be given a word, a drink from a sacred vessel, a waft of some magickal perfume or just a feeling of something being given over to you. Pathworkings, like dreams, involve characters other than the traveller.

These may be deliberately introduced or may spontaneously emerge. In many instances it is helpful to institute a guide or psychopomp in a pathworking. That is a figure, with a nature that corresponds to the area of the mindscape to be explored, that acts as a conductor for the whole or part of the pathworking. For differing pathworkings use different psychopomps; you will need to choose a character - be it an Egyptian deity, Greek hero or North American Indian spirit - that is suited to the particular area of the mindscape concerned. None of these entities is intended to become a life-long 'guide' or personal mentor, rather all have their uses depending on context.

Most psychopomps are aspects of the Mercurial archetype - in the respect that it is these forces which link, communicate and bridge the gaps between different areas of the self, or the conscious and unconscious. In general, it is best to avoid the whole psychopomp issue until such time as you have a more detailed knowledge of the esoteric doctrine of correspondences (next chapter). If such entities appear spontaneously, accept their reality within the context of the specific level of the mindscape, but remember to analyse your results in detail afterwards. The astral realm is easily molded by the individual and it may be that you are just projecting what you want to see onto an actual entity or that the whole thing could be total fantasy. The symbolism of the tarot will provide you with all the psychopomps you will require.

Induction

Read the following induction method and memorise the order in which the areas of the bodymind are induced to relax. Then try it yourself in your quiet room, to begin with try it as a relaxation exercise. If you are reading for another person, being read to, or have taped the induction, speak clearly, quietly, and use a relaxed smooth voice - don't rush the exercise.

Lie in the Shiva asana (if you wish to stretch any muscles do so, settle down).

Think about your feet, concentrate on your feet. Curl up your toes lightly and slowly let them go. Again curl up your toes and slowly let them go. Now your ankles; pull the whole of your feet up to point towards your chin, as far as they will go and, slowly, let them go. And again repeat; pull your feet up to point towards your chin as far as possible and relax, let them go...

Now your feet feel very heavy, sinking right down into the floor, just let the floor support them. Now think about your calf muscles, tighten all the calf muscles, until your legs feel stiff, then let them go. Relax and repeat. Feel, as before, the floor supporting the total weight of your calves.

Now think about your knees and the muscles around your knees, tighten all of them and let them go. Repeat and relax into the floor beneath you.

Now, from the waist to the sides of your feet, you feel heavy, just let the floor support you. and think about your stomach muscles. Contract them as hard as you can, release them. Repeat and relax them into the floor.

Think about your hands. Make a tight fist and really make them shake with tension and slowly let them go. And your shoulders, shrug them up to your ears and slowly let them go. Repeat and relax then into the floor.

From your neck to the sides of your feet you feel very, very heavy, sinking into the floor, just let the floor support you. Now think about your mouth, clench your teeth together and let them go. Repeat and relax.

Now the muscles of your eyes. Screw your eyes up until your faces is all pulled up. Slowly relax. Repeat and relax.

From the top of your head to the sides of your feet you feel heavy, comfortable and totally relaxed. Sink into the ground beneath you, allow it to carry all your weight.

Exercise

Experiment with writing your own pathworkings. Consult the texts listed in the bibliography. Try to follow the scheme given above. Try the following short pathworking.

Decide where you want to go first. You might go back to your old school, back into a dream you had the night before or into a place that has special meaning for you. Relax and follow the induction procedure. Now imagine yourself standing before your own front door. Make the image as clear as you can and step through the door into your desired location. Walk around and explore the landscape. Be aware of all the sensory information you obtain. Then, when you are ready, create the image of your own front door in front of you and return to your 'earth temple'.

Try 'practical' forms of this pathworking - perhaps taking you back to a particular location in order to find something that you have physically lost e.g an address book. Experiment with writing non-visual pathworkings. Imagine you are writing for a blind person, how would you construct the script? Investigate music which was written to convey a pathworking script in audio format.

The following pathworking is called the 'Journey to Understanding'. The imagery is based on the watery element, its' purpose is to allow you to understand the nature of cycle and flow as expressed by the water element. It will also give you the opportunity to learn how the water element unites the duality of negative and positive forces.

Relax your bodymind. Imagine that you are in a room, look around you. The room is warm and comfortable and you are seated on a deep sofa in front of an open fire. You are relaxed and receptive, listening, waiting for your favourite time of day. There are sounds of the hearth all around you; a kettle hissing quietly, a cat purring, the fire crackling softly. You feel warm arms around you, gentle but firm and strong and you smell the scent of fresh earth. You are looking out toward the corner of the room, and there, through a star-shaped window you see a crescent moon, upturned like a boat in the sky. There is a sudden wind, the fire leaps up and you find yourself in a silver boat, dark sky around you, floating down river. You feel that there is somewhere that you must go, although you do not yet know where. As you float down stream, you hear secrets whispered in your ears though you cannot quite catch the words, sometimes they sound like the water murmuring or the gentle hissing of the hearth you have left behind.

Down, along the river you travel, with the secret always in front of you, sometimes a little lonely and sad, but always going forward. On either side of you, you see rocks, crags and spires. On one side, is the night sky, mysterious, dark and fey, but very beautiful. Between the night shrouded rocks, waterfalls in shining cascades, you catch glimpses of dark cavern mouths and of strange silent people. Looking up you see outlined in the moonlight a unicorn, strong and graceful, horn erect, waiting for you. On the other side, the sun is shining brightly, between the rocks are bright flowers and strong, ancient trees. Cliffs rise up in the distance and on one you see a great stag, outlined in the sunlight, antlers raised high into the blue sky. The stag is formidable but you know that he is watching you along the way. You feel the strengths of either side, supportive, protective but never do you change direction or head to the shore. Fish jump in the water and a breeze blows, sometimes you catch the tang of salt in the breeze but it is soon gone.

The journey continues and you are a little tired, maybe wishing for home, but feeling always the strong, invisible arms around you pushing you gently forward, helping, guiding you on your way. Ahead and behind you, on the peaks of the distant mountains, burn beacons showing you your way. Along both banks you see people, beckoning, calling you ashore. Shall you stop, shall you wait? They are offering you food and drink, you feel suddenly thirsty and hungry, one figure holds a musical instrument. You are tempted by their company and long to hear a friendly voice but ahead of you lies the secret and you cannot wait. You continue on and the figures on the bank disappear behind you. You become aware that your hands are holding a silver chalice full of wine and that the boat is filled with fruits and bread. You hear sweet music carried in the wind and you eat and drink and feel refreshed, wondering why you did not notice these provisions before.

The smell of salt becomes stronger in the air, the wind blows you along faster and before long you can see the open sea. You lean over the edge of the boat and look into the deep, fathomless waters. You hear the music of the waves and distant voices, you hear one voice above the rest, speaking words only for you, words that you will always remember. And as you gaze at the sea which unites the lands of day and night, you begin to understand, and you plunge noiselessly, and without fear into the waters. The words of the voice stay with you as you sink down, comfortable and relaxed and find yourself seated in the comfort of the deep sofa, feeling strong, alive and greater in understanding.

Relax and become aware of the earth beneath you, relax and open your eyes, become aware again of your quiet room and return to your earth temple.

(Record all your results immediately). Notice the way statements, commands, open-ended descriptions and specific imagery are woven together to form a pathworking.

Reading Forms

There are many formats of reading that you may be asked for, or wish to experiment with. In the previous chapter we dealt with 'face to face' tarot reading, the wisdom of dealing with two clients simultaneously has already been discussed. If a couple 'emotionally involved' both require readings then read separately, ask them to talk to each other, and then, if necessary return to you to talk over their situation together. Similarly, two friends may wish to consult you together (possibly because one or both are nervous and seek 'safety in numbers'). You may arrange this by seating one in another room, or part of the room. Alternatively you may wish to ascertain how close their relationship is, and proceed if there are 'no secrets' between them. This presents the same problems as reading for any couple but may be necessary for your clients' confidence. (Incidentally, when referring to those emotionally/sexually involved with your client it is a good idea to use the word 'partner' in the reading. This can prevent embarrassment or misunderstanding as to their marital state or sexual preference. Whatever the situation, this is of no concern to you as the reader, but may upset the client if it is not handled tactfully).

One modern addition, to the use of the tarot is that you may wish, or be requested to audio tape the reading, or even to have it written down. Once again the choice is yours. As a reader you may find a tape recorder distracting and it is often the case that the client will automatically recall, perhaps some days after the reading, what you have said, therefore making any recording unnecessary. (In taking a written transcript of your words there is also a danger that the scribe will distort your meaning It is often not so much the words but rather the intonation of them which is important). Another possible variant is postal reading. As you may not have previously met the client, this requires a high level of reading skill and concentration. As you cannot gain immediate feedback the amount of information you require from your postal client will vary according to your personal needs. You may wish to ask for a photograph of the client and perhaps a letter from them in their own handwriting. If you have any knowledge of astrology you may wish to ask for their birth date, time and place to establish their sun and moon sign, this may help in selecting a significator card or in identifying which person in your reading is actually the client. With a postal reading you may also want additional information about what the client wants to know, although the information could be misleading If you intend to send your results to the client by post, keep a copy of the reading, both the cards you selected and your impressions from them.

Reading for Yourself

Reading for yourself is a far more exacting task than reading for another however difficult their situation. If you feel the need for guidance you may wish to contact a reputable reader, if however you have developed confidence in your own abilities, it can be both interesting (as an experiment), and useful (in terms of the information gained) to read for yourself. The key here is objectivity. You must maintain the open flow of perception to allow impressions from organised imagination to flow. You must be wary of confusing genuine intuition with impressions born of 'what you want to hear'. It is perfectly possible to read for yourself but to perform an accurate reading requires practice, perseverance and skill.

Reading Skill

Reading requires organisation of imagination. This may be likened to the way in which an abstract idea becomes manifest in a concrete form (much as an artist translates a feeling into a painted image). The human thought process is a combination of two mechanisms - logical thought and non-linear thought.

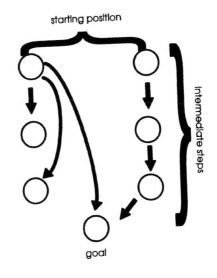

starting position

intermediate steps

goal

These two patterns of thought are often, erroneously, described as two systems which are utilised by the left and right hemispheres of the brain. In fact they are, as you will soon see from reading, two interwoven strands which will only constitute a single, full, mental process when seen together.

Reading the tarot involves being able to use these apparently opposed methods in unison. This is done by developing a kind of mental 'story board' of associated intuitional impressions, conceptual leaps and logical thought. You must learn to tell a story, guided by your intuition and expressed in a logical way to your client (or indeed yourself).

To begin your experimentation in reading try the following exercises.

Single Card Tales

Select a card, at random, from your deck. You may wish to try this exercise in your quiet room, having first relaxed your bodymind by whatever method suits you best. You may also wish to tape record what you say.

Look at the card then simply begin to produce a cameo story from the impressions you receive from it. The story itself may be whimsical, personal, highly descriptive or abstract. In any event let the ideas, associations and words flow. Don't try to analyse what you are saying and don't be afraid to say what comes into your mind, no matter how silly it may seem. Simply let go and allow your intuition to have full reign.

The Tarot Story

Repeat the above procedure with a number of cards (five is a good number to start with as this provides plenty of scope for ideas). Select the first card and begin your story, when you feel you need more information select another. Try to keep the story fluid, again don't feel self-conscious about this however funny, melodramatic or mundane the story may seem. Don't try to force your story into the mould of 'a reading' or attempt to obtain any astonishing revelations. The key here is to play, for it is by play that humans learn. One of the best ways to do this exercise is to imagine you are telling a story to a child using the cards as the visual accompaniment to the narrative. Better still, if you or a friend have a child who is old enough to listen, try telling them a story with the cards.

Word Association

Experiment with word association games. These may come in various forms and are often best if you can play them with other people. Try selecting cards rapidly one after another. Either tape record or write down, as soon as you see the card, a word which you associate with it. Don't limit yourself to repeating parrot fashion 'classical key-words' for each image. If the Knight of Cups brings chop suey to mind then say so. Remember in a reading that even the most outlandish impression may be of great importance to your client.

Having A Look

Try taking your cards out, at least once a week, just to 'have a look'. Again don't consciously try for startling information about the future. Just view the cards selected as being statements of where you are now. Record which cards you select and what impressions you get.

The simple exercises given above form the basis of reading skill. Learn to relax and not feel shy about saying what you feel. Begin to establish 'chains of thought', which are initiated by intuition but expressed by logic (so the client will understand your impressions).

The only real practice is doing, no amount of theoretical knowledge is going to allow you to read the tarot successfully.

Debriefing & Focusing

Tarot can be an exacting form of counselling, in that it falls outside of the usual net of counselling techniques. In terms of providing a methodology of listening and response, more standard forms of counselling can provide you with useful background information and ideas. However as 'tarot counsellors' you are using the extra 'sixth sense' (or perhaps a heightened and integrated form of the usual five). The counsellor, in the established sense, has empathy not sympathy with the client. As a reader, having access to more levels of information, there is a tendency to forget this distinction of relationship and become too involved with the client. This requires some care, both to maintain your own neutral objectivity with the client and to prevent (or at least be in charge of) any exchanges of 'subtle energy' between you. As we have said the tarot is a communication but this exchange exists on many levels other than the verbal. In the jargon of magick you are exchanging energy with your client; this can be a beneficial process to you both but in many cases you may find yourself inadvertently absorbing the unbalanced energy from your client or being drained of energy yourself. This occurrence should not be confused with the ever popular, but highly sensational phenomena of 'psychic vampirism'. In the vast majority of cases your client, particularly if they are under stress, will automatically draw energy from you, or 'unload' their energy onto you. This situation can provide a range of useful opportunities where you can 'transform' the energy flow between yourself and the client into a beneficial, flowing circuit of energy.

Central to magick is the notion that all the universe is formed of eternally moving, flowing energy (a view which physics has confirmed). No energy is itself good/evil or even negative/positive in the usual meaning of these terms. However you will often come across people whose' own energy cycles are unbalanced or lacking in some respect. By using the exercises given below you can develop methods of transmuting the energies emanating from your client and then return them in a more harmonious form. You may also evolve methods of preventing yourself from being 'drained' by the client.

In standard counselling forms it is usual, for the counsellor to have access to a support group to assist in 'de-briefing'. This helps the counsellor relax and leave the situation to prevent an 'emotional overload'. Whilst actual disclosures of a personal nature concerning your client should be avoided (particularly if you are dealing with people known to each other) it is acceptable to deal hypothetically or to discuss your own feeling about the work you have done with a close, supportive individual.

Transformation of Energy

There are many ways whereby energy can be drawn in from your client, transmuted in your own body and returned in a more harmonious form.

Colour Exchange
One of the easiest ways to transform energy is to imagine it as consisting of coloured light. Essentially the method consists of the following steps:

1) Absorption of energy from the client.

2) Internal transformation of energy into a usable form by the clients' bodymind.

3) Return of the clients' own energy to them but in an altered form.

To begin with practice exchanging energy with a being that already has a balanced energy flow - such as a tree.

Find a tree in your own locality. It should be fairly old and healthy. Place your hands on the trunk and relax your bodymind by breathing slowly and regularly. Then try to see energy entering your body via the left hand, passing through you and exiting your body through the right hand. According to magickal theory the right hand, in most people, directs energy outward and the left hand receives energy. Allow impressions to move through you, again record your results.

Try sensing your own energy circuit. Hold your hands a few centimetres apart and feel anything which passes between them (it is interesting to note that many belief systems suggest pressing the palms of the hands together in prayer or meditation. Thus creating a closed circuit of power to allow the individual to concentrate internally). Try various methods of transforming energy within yourself. You may wish to visualise the colours of energy changing; for example drawing in blue light with your left hand and imagining red energy being emitted from your right. You could imagine a prism or globe of white light situated in your own body which acts as a converter for energy.

In the context of a reading, you need not physically touch the client to do this. You could imagine a flow of energy existing between their eyes and yours, or perhaps between your bodies as a whole, using the cards between you as the medium through which the energy is transformed.

Containing Energy

To begin with it is important to stress that containing energy is not the same as withholding energy (a cup contains liquid to prevent it running away but is open to allow refilling or drinking). The first way to help maintain your own energy balance is to ensure that the physical components of your bodymind are well stocked with fuel (food) and that you are dressed in comfortable clothes and perhaps provided with a drink (you may end up doing a lot of talking!). The first way of conserving these 'subtle energies' is in the way you interrelate with the client; you must be understanding but not become wrapped up in their situation. The second way is to prepare yourself, psychically, for the reading. You will need to evolve a method that suits you best but it should follow a basic series of steps.

1) Relaxation of the bodymind complex.
2) Generation of a perimeter around the bodymind complex.
3) Construction of the perimeter so that it acts as a semi-permeable membrane (as in a cell wall).
4) Affirm your bodymind as the centre of the perimeter.

Most methods of doing this are based on the magickal notion that each body (be it animal, vegetable or mineral) is surrounded by an invisible but, with training, perceptible, field of energy - the aura.

1. Preparation: try this exercise initially in your quiet room. No special preparation is necessary, though you should perform whatever practices necessary to relax your bodymind. Imagine your body surrounded with an egg-shaped field of light. Experiment with various colours, blue (the sort of electric blue seen when electricity discharges in the air) is, for many people, the most effective colour to focus on. Concentrate on seeing/feeling this light until you can perceive its' existence without exerting conscious effort.

2. Mentally recognise that the aura around you will act as a semipermeable membrane, allowing energy to flow through both from you outward and inward but that any drain on your energy will be prevented and that any unbalanced energy will simply bounce off the auric field.

3. Focus on your bodymind and become aware of your breathing, still feeling the 'auric egg' around you.

To adapt this system you should experiment with other visualisations and see how effective they are. Thus you could imagine your breath forming a rainbow of colour around you, which is strengthened each time you breathe. You could even imagine your body becoming enveloped in a science fiction type space capsule. Remember that you are trying to

'centre' your energy not to lock it away to become isolated and stagnant.

Down to Earth

After you have finished your reading you will need to return to everyday reality; to put away your cards and make a definite stop. If you have followed the above procedures you may find that you are on something of a 'high' after reading. This occurs because, whilst reading, you will have entered a low-level trance state which will have a number of effects on your consciousness.

In order to return to earth, or 'ground' yourself, you must take account of both physical and psychological factors. When beginning a reading many readers light a candle which they then snuff out when the reading is completed, affirming that 'the session is over and done'. Afterwards let your mind focus on something less profound - watch T.V., go for a walk, do the washing up. De-briefing mentioned earlier, will help you in this respect. If you still find yourself 'drifting off' then you must take action. Even the low-level trance of tarot can cause problems if you don't keep your level of awareness under control. Make a definite termination of the reading - change your clothes and go out and dig the garden. If you are 'high' on the energy then do a simple relaxation exercise and then go and do something mundane. Physically it is wise to eat and drink after reading. You may well find that after a reading, you are thirsty. Again this is a physiological effect of low-level trance of your bodymind complex. You may also find that the peripheral areas of your body, hands and feet, become colder. A warm drink, such as tea or a small amount of alcohol combined with a little nutritious food is one of the best ways to 'ground out' the energy of the reading.

- # Taking the Tarot Inward

The following exercises are designed as centreing methods to help bring you back to earth, fully, and with as little shock as possible, after performing any of the more internalised practices you have encountered so far. The chapter also contains a self evaluation exercise and a short section covering what could be called 'magickal morality', concerning issues such as karma.

Centreing

There are a number of rituals which may be used to conserve your psychic energy and/or earth yourself before or after a given exercise. These practices will serve to re- vitalise your energies and to relax the bodymind complex.

Light Breathing

Seat yourself in a comfortable asana, be sure your spine is straight.

Relax your breathing to a steady rate and just spend a few moments becoming aware of your natural breathing. Imagine your breath as a white light flooding your body with brilliant illumination and spreading to every part of you, as you breathe in. Be aware of the light invigorating you, relaxing you, strengthening you.

Breathe out and image all the tension, and 'unbalanced' energy being expelled from your body. you may wish to, or spontaneously 'see', the exhaled air as being a sort of dirty, grey light which is forced out from all of your bodymind, not just the lungs. Continue until you feel totally relaxed and energised (or until you are both inhaling and exhaling white light). Stop the exercise and just become aware of the changes, if any, it has produced.

Sun Worship

This exercise is much the same as the one given above and is closely related to the certain practices in Tai C'hi Chuan.

Stand with your knees slightly bent and your feet facing forward about the width of your shoulders apart. Imagine the brilliant noonday sun above you as a globe of radiant, harmonious light. (If you can perform this exercise outside in real sunshine then so much the better.)

Let your arms fall naturally by your sides. Now as you inhale feel the light soaked air flooding into your whole body. Fill the lungs from their base upwards. As you breathe in raise, your arms upward, palms uppermost and outstretched until they are above your head, straightening your legs as you do so.

Breathe out and feel the energy flowing through you and back outward to the sun. Move your hands downward and gently, slowly bend your legs. Repeat as much as you like and relax. Be aware of any changes in your bodymind complex. Don't rush the movements or try to constrain your breathing to make the movements slow. The whole process should be natural and flowing, like the opening and shutting of a flower.

The Cross of Powers

This exercise can be used in many contexts. It is a very effective focusing method although it will probably need practice for you to get the most out of it.

The cross symbolism is derived from the Hebrew Qabalah (but predates that system). Orthodox Christianity, particularly Catholicism appropriated the cross symbol but failed to retain the esoteric meaning of it.

Stand or sit in a comfortable asana. Relax your breathing and keep it slow and regular throughout the exercise.

Raise your hands above your head with your hands palm to palm (as if praying). Imagine above you the quality of void, the unmanifest beginning of all things. This is the difficult part as you will have to feel rather than concentrate on one specific image or visualisation. Begin by visualising the night sky, infinite and silent above you.

Bring your hands down and touch your hands on your solar plexus. Feel now the energy of manifestation, or all creation. To help you try to imagine a scarlet, infinitely small core of energy (an atomic seed if you like). Be aware that you are connecting together the forces of chaos and manifestation within your bodymind.

Place the palm of your left hand on your solar plexus and, slowly move your right arm outward so that it is fully extended and at right angles to your body. Keeping the palm of your right arm open image the yin, negative, passive, feminine, forces of the universe to the right of you. You may wish to imagine the full moon in the night sky to give you a more concrete image until you can work simply by feeling these qualities.

Move your arm back, describing an arch, and rest your right hand, palm against your left shoulder. Your arm should lie across your breast so that the its' elbow is resting at the base of the right side of your ribcage. Become aware that you have just absorbed the negative forces in the universe (or 'Spirit passive' that is the harmonious matrix formed by the interaction of the elements of water and earth) into your bodymind.

Keep your right arm where it is and repeat this process with your left arm. This time imagine you are interfacing with the yang, positive, masculine, active forces in the universe (or you may wish to begin this practice by imagining the sun in a deep blue sky). Move your arm in an arch until it is across your breast (palm flat against your right shoulder, elbow at the base of the left side of your ribcage). Become aware that you are drawing in the positive forces in the universe into your bodymind (i.e 'Spirit active' - the balanced matrix of air and fire). You are now standing in what is called the 'Osiris Risen Position' (the Egyptian God Osiris is often depicted with arms crossed over his breast, usually holding crook (symbol of the passive forces in the universe) and flail (symbolising the active powers in the universe).

You are now the 'field of operations' within which all the forces in the universe exist, in a harmonious, but changing state - i.e 'dynamic equilibrium', and you both contain and are contained within. In this exercise you are 'invoking' the six forces of the universe - that is chaos, form, Earth & Water, Air & Fire (corresponding to height, depth, North, West, East and South respectively).

Knowledge Evaluation

Write down the events of the last two weeks and how your self development played a part in what happened. Record the results you got from certain exercises but include dreams, personal events, changes in attitude and at least three totally mundane events. If you are covering the work properly then you should be finding that your 'magickal consciousness' extends into both the sublime and ridiculous aspects of your life.

Take a large sheet of paper and a number of coloured pens or similar. Draw a large circle on the paper. This is your own disk or pentacle. Try in symbolic form, words or any other form you wish (such as collage or the interrelation of different colours) to express all your knowledge on this pentacle. It may take numerous attempts but you should end up with a mandala-like device, a complete image, or interwoven set of images which express you - your knowledge, experience and understanding. This is a very useful exercise, so try it. Once you have finished put the disk somewhere conspicuous, perhaps on the wall in your quiet room. Over the course of the next month, consult it occasionally. What changes would you make to it now? At the end of the month re-draw your disk from a new perspective. (The following diagram shows one example but there is no 'right' way to do it and your pentacle should be totally individual.

Ask yourself the following questions and if you are letting things slip then go back to using these foundational techniques.

Are you still taking your cards out and 'having a look' at them?

Are you still practicing the relaxation techniques taught earlier?

Are you referring to other books or are you taking this one as 'gospel'?

Are you still observing your environment to the level that you should?

Are you becoming bound up in a complex, confused web of ideas, or are you allowing yourself 'space to feel'?

Are you still keeping, and analysing your diary properly?

Elementary knowledge

Draw up four columns in your magickal diary. Title each one with the name of one of the four elements.

Without referring to any texts, write down answers to each of the following questions within each column.

1) What suit in the Minor Arcana refers to each element?

2) What colour would you ascribe to each element?

3) What animal or 'Kherub' is attributed to each element (remember that in most decks these four animals are depicted in Atu XXI 'The Universe')?

4) In the Court cards which characters show the 'pure form' of each of the four elements (i.e fire of fire, water of water, air of air and earth of earth)?

5) Name one object in the room you are sitting which could be ascribed to each element?

6) Which single word do you think would best sum up the nature of each elemental power?

7) To what compass direction is each element usually ascribed?

8) Name one mythological figure (i.e a god, hero, demon or whatever) that you feel is related to each element.

9) Name an event in human life which you feel is under the auspice of each element.

10) Mark in, using the symbols '-' for negative and '+' for positive, the quality of each element.

Check your results and in each case don't just accept that an answer is 'right' or 'wrong' but ask yourself why you wrote what you wrote.

Morals and Magick

Magick is both an art & science and cannot be pigeon-holed neatly into the boxes of religion, philosophy, self-development, psychological technique or science. Magick itself does not seem to have any defined, immovable creed, as science or orthodox religion does. This is hardly surprising for magick is, literally, in all things, and no external dogma can be imposed as 'right'. Magick is the nature of the universe and is therefore totally amoral. In magick there is nobody to tell you what to do - no god, no devil - there is only you!

This can present a problem to the individual. Without a creed to define how one should and should not act then how should one act ? The answer this is simple, to quote the central theme of Taoist thought 'do nothing that is not according to nature and all will be achieved'. The only real way of working out what humans 'ought to do' is to become part of, and understand on all levels, (not just the conscious intellectual) the nature of the universe and to act according to the principles of that system.

Modern magickal theory (during the past fifty years) has made much of the principle of Karma. Karma seemed to offer a philosophy rooted in 'cosmic law' which could directly apply to the way humans act - whether or not one should rob banks, murder their mothers, eat meat or heal the sick. The difficulty in understanding Karma, is that it has become an isolated idea to be toyed with at an intellectual, philosophical nature; thus it has devolved into various silly creeds.

The word Karma itself is derived from Sanskrit and may be approximately translated into English as 'Action'. All the universe is action (i.e a complex interwoven tapestry of processes - from the millisecond cycles of sub-atomic particles, to the immense periods of galactic rotation) and all action supposes a cause and an effect, or to be more accurate an infinite chain of causes and effects of which there are no finite limits. Many who have written on the subject of magick and morality see karma as a sort of cosmic judicial system where if one does something 'good' then one is rewarded, and if one does something 'bad' then one is punished as in a patriarchal religious system. The universe/magick is amoral. How can any act be good or bad? Each action is not one cause and effect but an infinite string of situations. The process of karma as an action/reaction principle, cannot be understood properly without the understanding of your own 'inner nature' or True Will.

The True Will is the natural course of the individual through the universe, it is the line of least resistance through the cosmos which the individual must discover and attempt to pursue (rather like the path of least resistance, through which water flows due to gravity or electricity to earth). The pivotal point of magick is discovering your own True Will.

The True Will can be imagined as being a vertical line on which a series of beads has been strung. Each bead represents an experience or set of events. Karma may be described as being a force or pressure which exists around this 'line of least resistance'. The conscious mind of the individual is often at odds with the path of the True Will, perhaps wishing to side-step one of the 'experience beads' which lie along that line. The more the individual attempts to deviate from the path of the True Will, the greater the pressure exerted by the 'karmic force', and the more dramatic will be the 'kick-back' effect. This is in contrast to the 'New Age' theory that if you follow your own path 'perfectly' then nothing painful will happen to you or that you never enter any difficult situations. The True Will and Karma are inherent in the universe, and the individual must experience the Apophis stage if real learning is to take place. In the final analysis these are natural processes, you cannot avoid dirty hands or physical death by adhering to the path of the True Will. If a mothers' child is attacked, the natural law of the situation is that the mother defends her child - there is no time to start worrying about 'karmic consequences' or mysterious 'principles'. The fact that the mothers' child was attacked is the result of a complex series of causes and effects both to her, her child and the attacker. Supposing that she is getting her just desserts in such a situation is just moral cowardice.

The True Will is such that, if everybody followed their own path, no conflicts would arise of a purely destructive kind, between individuals. To understand this you can consider the path of the True Will as being like the orbital path of a star. Each star orbits and exchanges gravitational waves and light with other stars, it does not collide with others unless it has strayed from its' natural orbit. So how do these natural principles apply in everyday life and, more particularly, in magick?

Being an aware human being means having power - power to harm or heal, yourself and others. In the context of the tarot you have access to tremendous power, especially as a diviner. If a person comes to you, having recently lost a loved one, they may very well ask you if you can 'contact' their departed relative with the cards. To the unscrupulous this presents an opportunity to bleed their client dry of money to pay for an imaginary power. You may be asked to 'do a spell' to lay a curse on, or heal somebody. There is no use thinking to yourself 'well that's not a problem, I can't do that anyhow', the fact is that, whatever your abilities, you do have the potential to do so! Just as you have the potential to jump in a car and run somebody over deliberately or heal them by using medicinal or counselling skills.

In situations which are not governed by immediate action/reaction (such as the instance of the mother defending her child) you have the opportunity to think about what you could/should do. Essentially, you must be certain that whatever you do is looked at through the perspective of the four elements. That is:

Earth: What are the social, cultural and practical constraints or possibilities? How will your actions affect the physical level of reality?
Water: What emotional factors exist?
Air: What intellectual factors exist?
Fire: How does the situation relate to your own drive (True Will)?

There are no easy solutions, you must be ready to face every possibility but, the key is 'be true to your own nature' with the parallel process of 'know thyself' being always in mind.

You can never know exactly how anything you do will affect the rest of the universe (and, by inference, yourself). You can only act according to your own nature as best you are able.

Take the opportunity to consider the power you have at your disposal, both as a magickian and as a human being as a whole. Remember nothing is inherently evil or good - your own hands are able to maim someone or save them from death. 'Know thyself' means more than just playing around with ideas in your own head, it is an ongoing process and must relate to your dealing with others not just by what you think but also by what you do.

- # Magick in the Air

The nature of air is that it divides (in the form of space), serves to set up logical 'chains of thought' and is thus associated with communication (just as our words, which are a logical form of communication, are transmitted through the air medium).

In the tarot, the suit ascribed to the element of air is Swords. Blades are objects which divide one thing into two - air is the element which governs the analytical processes. Analysis is vital to your development - discerning fact from fiction and the underlying factors and results, especially in your magickal record.

Understanding the element of Air means being able to break down any given situation, belief or experience into its constituent parts. It also means being able to formulate a sequence of ideas, images or concepts which can then be used to re-unite that which has been divided. Language is an 'airy' process; the universe is divided into a series of words which are formed by dividing noise into a string of basic sounds, often characterised in writing by a set of symbols. Logical chains are made of these sounds (or characters denoting sounds) which are used to build up a system of communication. Spoken and written languages are limited to cultural, historical and linguistic constraints (e.g a person who speaks only English cannot understand a German speaker by spoken words). Magick has a common language in the form of the archetypal units of self which are expressed in the 78 cards in the tarot - each of these units may be described by using a system known as correspondences.

Correspondence attributes both objects and ideas to the four elements. No one correspondency can sum up all the features of any given force. The rationale of correspondences is quite simple - that certain forces, which cannot be themselves perfectly described, may be expressed by associations; e.g colours, metals, animals, gemstones, scents etc.

The practical application of correspondence is diverse. In the context of pathworking, it initially serves to provide a series of images which will help you write a script that will pertain, as accurately as possible, to the desired level of the mindscape. In other words a 'chain of correspondence' serves as a series of sign posts to guide you into, and through, any given level of the Self. Correspondence is the practice of 'post pathworking analysis'. Correspondences can be so intimately interrelated to the archetypal forces in the Self that, by observing the imagery you encounter in a pathworking, it is possible to ascertain just how 'pure' the experience has been.

All symbolism exists, or is 'true' at various levels of being. The reality of any given correspondence can thus be described as existing on one of the following levels.

Level	Title	Example
1	Conscious Cognitive:	learned meaning or association, such as a traffic sign, or written character denoting specific sound or meaning.
2	Personal	An association based on personal (often childhood) memory, such as associating a particular perfume with ones' mother.
3	Cultural	From the experience of ones' own culture, or ethnic group, such as associating the symbol of the cross with the godform of Jesus.
4	Racial	Symbolism inherited from the genealogical background of the individual, such as an American having a deep affinity with harp music through his Welsh ancestry.
5	Archetypal	The basic fabric of the unconscious, common to all people (and many mammals), such as the symbolism of the 'serpent god'.

As with all models of reality levels, these symbolic groups blur into one another. The image of 'the vampire' exists as the antihero of many

Hollywood movies, within the folklore of Africa and as an image of the archetype which Jung referred to as 'the Shadow'.

Certain symbols, in the sense of units which describe the central archetypal forces of self, exist at different level. There are a set of correspondences which will apply at most levels for most people - these are set down in the form of another model of the universe, known as the Qabalah.

The Qabalah, or 'Tree of Life' provides one of the most comprehensive maps of inner and outer reality commonly available in modern magick. Over the long and often concealed history of the Qabalah it has been depicted in many ways; the most commonly used form today is based on what is called the 'Lurianic Scheme' (developed by the sixteenth century Jewish mystic Isaac Luria).

As you can see from the diagram overleaf the whole of the tarot system fits neatly into the Qabalah (or, perhaps, the Qabalah flows out of the tarot - historically it is almost impossible to extricate these two threads). Briefly, the spheres in the diagram are akin to the Chakras in Asian magick and are known as Sephiroth (Sephira in the singular) - a word which has much the same meaning as chakra. The lines or paths between the Sephiroth represent the paths of energy which flow between each sphere. The depth of symbolism contained within the Qabalah is infinite. Understanding this network of correspondences can take lifetimes but the there is no virtue in memorising great lists of associated symbols but appreciating the 'inner nature' of each archetype and thereby discovering the correspondences for yourself.

On an intellectual level it is worth equipping yourself with at least a little Qabalistic theory and consulting at least two books on correspondence, (see bibliography). Despite the apparent rigidity of the Qabalistic model, the whole system is designed to represent change (or magick). The Tree of Life is much more akin to a flow chart rather than a static filing system.

There are many processes which the Qabalah describes and in learning about this system, it is far more beneficial to become aware of this pattern of flux and flow rather than memorising long strings of correspondences.

Try the following exercises to help you understand how the Qabalistic system operates.

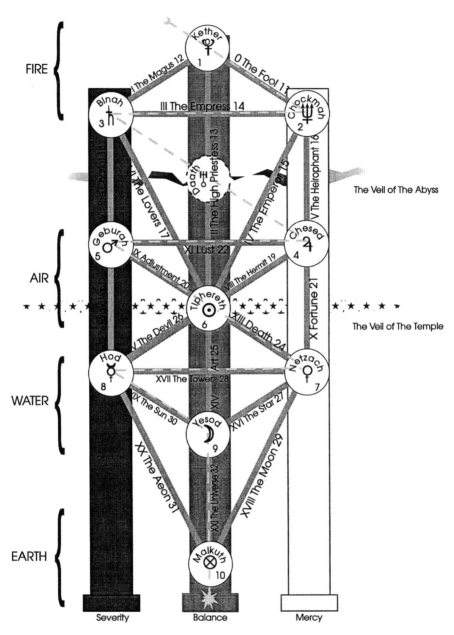

FIRE

AIR

WATER

EARTH

Kether
1

I The Magus 12

0 The Fool 11

Binah
3

III The Empress 14

Chockmah
2

II The High Priestess 13

Daath

The Veil of The Abyss

V The Hierophant 16

IV The Emperor 15

V The Lovers 17

Geburah
5

XI Lust 22

Chesed
4

IX Adjustment 20

VII The Hermit 19

Tiphereth
6

X Fortune 21

The Veil of The Temple

V The Devil 26

XIII Death 24

Art 25

Hod
8

XVII The Tower 28

Netzach
7

XIX The Sun 30

XIV

XVI The Star 27

Yesod
9

XX The Aeon 31

XXI The Universe 32

XVIII The Moon 29

Malkuth
10

Severity

Balance

Mercy

Qabalah - The Tree of Life

Making the Tree by Tarot.

In one sense the tarot may be seen as a Qabalistic map in 'kit form'.

Take your own cards and lay them out as per the diagram above, perhaps over a drawing of the tree on a large sheet of paper.

Fan out the Ace cards on Kether, and so on for each Sephira. Place each Major Arcana card on the respective path, include Cards on their respective Sephira also.

Now you have added the symbolism of your own tarot, and more importantly, what you know about each card, to the Qabalistic 'floor plan'.

Now consider the following, with reference to the symbolism you have in front of you.

I) The Qabalah may be divided into three major areas; the left hand pillar, the right hand pillar and the central pillar. These pillars are known by various names, the symbolism is thus:- the left hand pillar - passive energy, yin, negative, feminine, darkness, the right hand pillar - positive energy, yang, positive, masculine, light, the middle pillar - dynamic equilibrium between the other two forces. Look at the grouping of the cards and see if you can ascertain how the symbols interrelate in this sense.

II) The Tree of Life is unlike a physical tree in that its' root is at Kether, the 'top', and the termination of its' branches in Malkuth, the 'bottom'. Each sphere of the Qabalah represents an increasingly dense manifestation of energy as it moves from top to bottom (often referred to as the Lightning Flash). Again look at the way the cards fall across each Sephira. See if you are able to ascertain how this flow of energy occurs.

(N.B. This doctrine is often, wrongly, described as the 'Fall' of man from grace, spirit into matter or whatever. Spirit is a function of matter, not an opposite of it.)

III) A corresponding 'upward' flow of energy is found in the way the paths operate. This flow is described as the path of the Serpent of Wisdom. Consider the way the cards fall, where and how this flow operates.

115

Plotting the Real

Try plotting a system, whatever system you are most conversant with, on the Qabalistic diagram. The following example is given by Z'ev ben Shimon Halevi in his book 'Kabbalah'.

Don't worry about 'being right', take your time and consider your attributions according to what you know about the Qabalah.

Chaining Correspondences.

From the way your cards fit on to the Qabalistic diagram you may develop a clear picture of each area of the tree represents.

Try figuring out the attributions of incenses, perfumes, sounds, feelings etc., just as you did with the elements, to the spheres and paths of the tree.

For example: the element of Fire appears in the natural world in three main forms, as sparks (such as those generated by hitting flint stone), regular fire (as in the sun) and electrical fire (lightning). Since the sphere of Tiphareth is related, astrologically, to the Sun you could ascribe the regular or 'yellow' fire to it. Sparks could be ascribed to the sephira of Geburah which is ruled by the violent, sporadic force of Mars, and electrical fire to Chesed which is ruled by Jupiter who was the legendary god of lightning and thunder. Try analysing in increasing depth all your attributions; e.g.: traditionally the 30th path which is accorded Atu XIX 'The Sun' is ascribed the incense of Frankincense. This gum has a warm odour, grows in warm climates and was in biblical myth offered to Jesus who is a solar deity (i.e he dies and is reborn, just like the sun) - thus the attribution is, logically, very satisfactory. In most cases an attribution based on conscious 'common sense' will be valid in the 'irrational' depths of the unconscious also.

Checking your Pathworkings

The relative level and accuracy of a pathworking can be checked using a system drawn from the Qabalah called the 'key scales'. These are lists of colours which seem to prevail at certain areas in the mindscape. By using

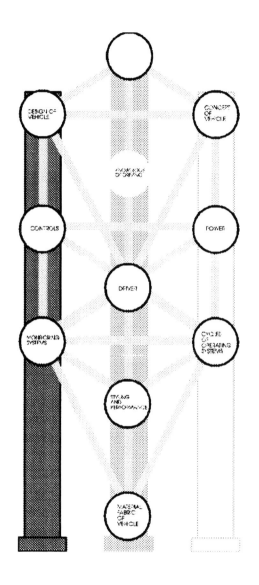

the key scales, you may check the depth to which you have gone in your unconscious. Generally, the closer the pathworking gets you to the core of the required area in the mindscape the less conscious imagery surfaces and the more the key scales apply. For instance, it would be unlikely that a fire orientated pathworking would bring you to an area in your mindscape full of fountains, rivers and placid aquatic entities unless your conscious mind was confusing the issue. Each path and sephira is ascribed four predominant colours. These are related to the four Court cards and their symbolism as representatives of the sixteen 'sub- elements'. They are listed in at the back of the book. Don't just accept these correspondences as correct but be prepared to use them as a general standard against which to judge your innerworld explorations until your have more experience. Try the following exercises and then the pathworkings that follow:

Suspending Belief

Take something you believe in such as 'nuclear disarmament is important', or 'the earth goes round the sun'. Now sit down and really think about your belief. Why do you hold it? What factors led to its' development? Why is it important to you? Spend a week trying to suspend your belief. If somebody asks you if you think eating meat is wrong and you previously considered that it was, argue the reverse of your original belief. Consider your results and whether your belief has changed or modified. You will have a better understanding of the fact that there are always many facets to every issue.

Paradoxical Ideas

Try considering two apparently contradictory ideas simultaneously. E.g consider the contrast between human freedom and slavery, mass starvation and cordon bleu cuisine, the vastness of space and the sub-atomic particle. See if you can detect and pinpoint where these opposing ideas are unified. You should become more aware of the nature of paradox, the subjectivity of 'truth' and increase your analytical ability.

Vigilance in Speech

Select a word or phrase that you commonly use and remove it from your speech for at least a week. Words such as 'I' or habitually repeated phrases such as 'actually' are the best choices. Make a note of each time you break your vow and under what circumstances. Don't replace one word with another but simply drop the word, and the concepts associated from it, from your vocabulary. (To do this exercise properly you should add an extra day to the duration of your practice each time you forget to discipline your speech.)

Breadth of Vision
Take time to seek out knowledge of yourself and your universe without concentrating solely on books about magick. Films, computer systems, novels, concerts, plays - all present you with opportunities to learn and experience more.

Mindfulness of Life
Take a few hours alone and perform some simple task such as washing the car, cleaning the house or taking a bath. Make a conscious effort to take things slowly, perform all your actions at half your usual speed or less. Think about each part of your task in detail, e.g.: 'now I am turning on the tap anti-clockwise, now I'm testing the temperature of the water with my hand' etc.. Think also about your sensations, 'now I'm feeling the wetness of the water and the slippery surface of the soap' etc.. When thoughts arise in your mind which are unrelated to your task simply acknowledge them and return to what you are doing. Pay attention to what is going on both internally and externally.

Divided Meditation
Go to your quiet room and take some time to relax your bodymind. Place your tarot deck, face down in front of you (shuffle them if you feel it necessary). Consider the deck as the whole of you, all the elements which make up your bodymind complex.

Now select a card and place it in front of you, then choose another from the pile and place it by the side of the first card you have selected. Consider the relationship between the two archetypes you have chosen. Select two more cards and consider the relationship between the cards on the left, the cards on the right, the new set of cards together and the top left/bottom right and top right/bottom left cards. Imagine that each interrelationship emulates the interaction of these forces within you (in the largest sense of 'you'). Continue to lay out the cards until you feel the relationships getting too complex to understand, lay out two more cards and just become aware of the pattern you have formed. Record the cards you have drawn and repeat the exercise at least four times noticing any changes. As you will see from this exercise you have automatically obtained a complete series of psychopomps in the form of the archetypal forces depicted in each card.

Pathworkings

The Golden Temple

This is a very short pathworking more akin to a visual meditation than anything else. This exercise can be easily adapted to allow you to examine many facets of your self. Relax your bodymind complex, focus on your breathing.

Imagine that you are climbing up a steep hill, up a staircase of many steps carved into the rock. At the top, there is a temple. There are four doors into the temple, select one of them and walk through it.

You find yourself in a room, empty of furniture but with walls covered with shelves full of books or scrolls. Take one of the documents from the self and stand in the centre of the room where a ray of sunshine falls on you from a skylight. Read the text and discover the answer to your question!

(Remember not to put too much store into what you might read in the temple. Do not ignore what you find but perhaps take messages informing you that you are the new messiah with a pinch of salt!)

Qabalistic Pathworking

The following is an example of a pathworking using the symbolism of the path which links the sephiroth of Tiphereth and Binah. This path corresponds to Atu VI 'The Lovers'.

The energies depicted here are those related to the zodiac sign of Gemini (ascribed to Atu VI) and the symbol of the Sword (the Hebrew letter associated with this path is 'Zain' which, literally translated, means 'a sword'). Most of the symbolism should be self-evident. Essentially, this path is one which comprehends the nature of the analysis/ communication/ synthesis symbolism of the Air element. It links the sun (the centre of the solar system and the life-giving force which animates the earth) with Saturn, the most distant, slow moving and darkest of the ancient planets. The 'lesson' of this path will form at different levels for different people.

Pathworking from Tiphereth to Binah using the Path of the Lovers

Relax your bodymind and focus your attention on the area of your heart chakra. Feel the Air flowing through your lungs, ebbing and flowing. Listen to the regular pulse of your heart. Take a few moments to become aware of these rhythms.

Now imagine a disk in front of you, a vast, bright disk of yellow light. This is the doorway of the Sun - make the visualisation firm and step through it...

You find yourself in a room, it has six sides and its' walls and contents are coloured with the bright tones of the sun in Summertime.

As you investigate the room, you see in one wall a doorway which you had not noticed before. Looking more closely you can see a symbol emblazoned upon it: it is a symbol from 'The Lovers' card and you know that this is the door through which you must begin your journey.

As you walk through the door, you find yourself in a fertile, green landscape. There are no other buildings visible but in the distance you see a looming range of mountains about which eagles circle, in the brilliant azure skies. There is a path which leads away from the temple, from which you have emerged, winding its' way through the valley. Two vast stone sphinx-like creatures stand sentinel on either side of the road, you pass beneath their shadows, feeling a strange cold, tingling sensation as you do so.

You walk along the pathway. As you do so you notice the animals and plants along the route: magpies chatter in the trees, deer peep shyly from the bushes, fabulously coloured orchids and berries grow here also.

Now, as you move further through the valley you notice that the breeze is becoming stronger, the leaves on the trees rustle and the birds and animals disappear from sight. Before you, much closer now, rise up two great black crags of rock and away to either side lie the long walls of a mountain range.

As you follow the path, it begins to ascend the foothills. The vegetation around you gives way to bushes and long tufts of grass swaying in the wind. Before you is a curious formation of rock, or perhaps it is a building. A silvery yellow cone which juts out of the earth and resting upon the top of the pinnacle is a sword. And you know the sword is for you.

As you stand at the base of the column you feel the wind whipping around you, yet there seems no way to grasp your prize. The surface is smooth and climbing it is impossible. All the while the gust of wind become stronger and as you stand at the base of the cone, you feel the wind begin to lift you upward. Your weight shrinks away and you are as light as a feather, you are lifted up and up, spiralling around the cone towards the sword at its' tip but without fear. The wind seems to hold you tenderly in its' grasp like a mother, supporting, carrying your weight. Reach out your hand and take the sword, it is part of you.

And, as you grasp the weapon it seems to glow with an inner light and you find yourself slipping back towards the earth. But now you find you have been lifted over the mountains and are standing at the shore of a vast, deep ocean.

You become aware of a strange figure standing beside you, dressed in a robe of many different colours. The figure speaks to you - listen to the words. As you hear them they seem, to come as much from you as from your companion and you understand that the powers of your intellect must be fused with the other powers within you. With the sword still in your hand you walk to the edge of the sea.

You raise the sword in your hands and cast it out into the air, for a moment it spins over the surface and then plunges into the water. You feel sorry to see it go and turn around - the figure you spoke to you is gone but where it was, point downwards into the earth stands your sword now glowing even more brightly than before. And upon the pommel you notice a jewel which burns golden yellow like the sun. As you look at it, it grows until it forms a doorway through which you can return, still remembering and understanding what has happened to you in this strange realm. Step through the doorway and become aware of the brilliant light gently pulsating in your heart. Be aware of the movement of the air through your lungs and that your whole body is the sword in your dream.

Relax and open your eyes.

✩ Spreads & Sequences

This chapter will cover some of the major spread structures used in tarot divination and suggest means by which you can formulate your own spreads. Experiment with the spreads and techniques given below but don't be fooled into thinking that any particular layout is right.

Touching the cards

There are two schools of thoughts concerning the touching of the cards - the first suggests that only the owner of the deck should handle their cards and the second suggests that, while initially, it is better to keep your cards to yourself, later they may be handled by others with relative impunity.

As the reader, you must decide which of these is better; within the context of a reading for another person we would suggest that you, the reader, should shuffle and deal the cards. If the querant shuffles the cards they may be unconsciously projecting an imagined problem onto the reading which, will distract you from the real situation.

A comparatively new development (as far as we can ascertain) is an assumption that the meaning of any one card is changed by the way in which it falls, with reference to the reader. If a card falls 'inverted' (i.e upside down from the readers' point of view - also referred to as 'ill-dignified' or 'reversed') then its' meaning is reversed. Thus, according to this system, Atu XIX 'The Sun' means 'material happiness' whereas the same card 'reversed' means 'failure'. This idea is inconsistent with the system itself, the cards only have meaning, either intrinsically or in conjunction with others, by the intuitive ability of the reader - therefore the 'upright' or 'invertedness' of any card does not have meaning in itself - it is the readers' own interpretation that counts. No card has a set meaning: Atu XIX could just as easily refer to the querents' car, mother or psychological state as 'material happiness', to suppose an instant reflection of a cards' 'particular meaning' by the cards position is to misunderstand the whole nature of tarot divination. There may be occasions where a cards' inversion may have significance but this should be judged by your own intuition. (This point is important - at different times, in different situations the same card can have many different even opposing meanings. Students with books which give precise definitions of each card find their readings difficult to interpret until they break away from the limitations of the text they are using.) The last point in debunking the theory of 'reversed cards' is that it is suggested that when a card is inverted that its' energy is twisted, unbalanced, or negative. Negative is a description of polarity (all energy must have polarity, to be energy) and is in no way the same as 'evil'. The whole issue implies that a reversed card is somehow wrong, sinister, evil, and is a superstitious shadow stemming from the misinterpretation of duality in moralistic terms.

Other notions of the Tarot include the turning of the cards with the left hand, never laying the cards out face upward, always keeping the pack in a particular order etc.. There are no inviolate laws to govern these choices of technique.

The Use of Spreads

To return to our analogy of the tarot cards acting as letters in the alphabet, the spread may be seen as the grammar of the tarot language. A spread is designed to assist the reader in seeing the specific relationship between the cards selected. In the initial stages of learning the Tarot, spreads provide a useful method of seeing the way in which the forces flow between each card selected, to form the whole (i.e the reading).

Spreads are a tool for assisting the organisation of the imagination, like the cards, they are not 'magickal' in themselves any more than a hammer and chisel are 'artistic' unless they are in the hands of a skilled sculptor. In the context of divination, the most obvious spread to choose would be a 'linear time spread'.

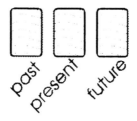

This depicts: Past: Present and Future. For an experienced reader these three cards may provide a key of sufficient potency to unlock all manner of intuitional responses. However, in many cases three cards will not provide a sufficient inspiration. To assist further inspiration, cards may be introduced which are intended to outline certain forces, which have a bearing on the querent.

There are a number of important considerations to bear in mind with relation to the description of spreads. Spreads exemplify the fact that cards themselves (in divination) only have meaning in terms of their relation, to other cards and as keys to your own organised intuition. Thus, in a spread, you may see a card position being described as 'environmental influence'; you may find your intuition is automatically keyed by the card in the respect of the function of the card; i.e. you intuit a series of environmental factors affecting the client from the card. In many cases you may feel the need of more information. If you do there are two options. The first is to consider the card in relation to the others in the spread and focus your attention on organising your intuition to pertain to environmental factors faced by the client. In this instance, the card in the 'environmental' position acts rather like a figurehead for the whole of the reading - which you will be interpreting from the perspective of the figurehead card. (In other words whatever aspect of the clients' situation you are considering, you will be using the card which occupies the relevant position in the spread, as your 'central key' but will derive your intuition from the spread as a whole.)

The second method is to lay out other cards near the card you are focusing your attention on. To use our language analogy again this is rather like taking a word and learning more about it by using a Thesaurus (the other cards) to establish its meaning. If you intend to use a set spread you will soon see that the mark of an effective spread is that you will not have to pull out other cards. The framework of the spread will be such that there will be sufficient 'keys' available for you to build up a clear picture of any aspect of the clients' situation, without drawing on more and more cards.

As tarot divination is about relation, it is important that, if you use a set spread, you begin by turning all the cards over in order to see all the patterns of interrelation in your reading. The following are examples of commonly used spreads with information on their structure and use. Try each of them out, research others and formulate your own (perhaps creating a hybrid from a detailed understanding of two of more established methods). Experiment with them both in reading for yourself and for others.

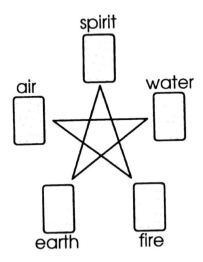

This spread is based on the interaction of the four elements and their equal combination in the form of Spirit. Each card can be seen as being the figurehead of the whole reading, representing the manifestation of the denoted elemental quality as related to the level of the reading. The Spirit card serves, again in conjunction with all the others, to represent the 'overture' or general aura of the reading taken as a whole. To explain this more exactly, here are two instances where the same reading can be used on two different levels.

Employment level
Earth: financial security, income.
Water: emotional relationships with others at work.
Air: possibilities to change and develop within the context of employment.
Fire: career situation and possibilities.

Bodymind level
Earth: physical health.
Water: emotional state (such as that shown in dreams).
Air: intellectual status.
Fire: drive or Will (or lack of it).

You need only to use these five cards to see both these levels, or any other implied levels of meaning. Use your common sense make it applicable at the desired level. Thus, if you have a feeling of great progress, change, and movement from the reading, this could be interpreted as being a physical change of job and perhaps location. On another level, it may be obvious that the querent is emerging from a psychological rut and is become more open to possibilities for growth and change in their own life.

The Ten Card Spread

This spread is also known as the 'Celtic Cross' or 'Solomons' Circle'. According to Stuart R.Kaplan this method dates back several centuries and is one of the oldest documented divinatory spread. The cards are laid out in the following manner:

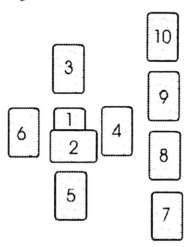

The descriptions of the placings for each card are self explanatory but the following will give you a more detailed picture of the spreads' structure. In any established spread the organisation of the cards can only give you information. Your instincts and knowledge must be the qualifying factor:

Card 1 - Present Position: this shows the querent in the present. It represents the immediate influences and atmosphere surrounding the questioner at present. This card forms the significator.

Card 2 - Immediate Influences: This card crosses the significator and demonstrates the main events which are imminent in affecting the querent.

Card 3 - Goal: This card crowns the significator and represents the querents' goal or aim from the perspective of the present circumstances.

Card 4 - Distant past: this placing shows, broadly, the underlying factors which have led the querent to their present situation.

Card 5 - Recent Past Events; this card, placed beneath the significator, represents the immediate past influences on the querent. It may also refer to events in the clients' life which have been so potent that they still influence the life of the subject.

Card 6 - Future Influences: this card shows, broadly, the general trend of future events that will affect the querent.

Card 7 - The Questioner: shows the attitude of the querent to the past, present and future circumstances surrounding them. This card provides an extension of the ideas developed in Card 1.

Card 8 - Environmental Factors; shows the physical, usually inter-personal, factors acting on the querent.

Card 9 - Inner Emotions: this placing sheds light on the hidden hopes, fears, desires and attitudes of the questioner - emotions which may be hidden either by others from the querent, or by the querent themself.

Card 10 - Final Result; shows the final outcome of the various factors already considered, provided events and influences appear in the ways the reading has suggested.

A spread such as this is similar to a simple flow chart, with a definite beginning and ending. Methods such as this may prove useful for examining simple problems but may tend to gloss over more subtle levels in the divination. The ten card spread is a very useful system, so practice it and, even if you don't have cause to use it, it will provide 'another string to your bow'.

Triangle Spread

Also known as the 'Pyramid Spread', this method has many uses, our first example is based on the 'biorythmic' system.

This spread is concerned with the whole nature of the person and, by intuitively analysing that nature, extrapolating predictive information.

The cards are arranged in the form of a triangle with its apex at the bottom (although it could just as well be at the top) thus:

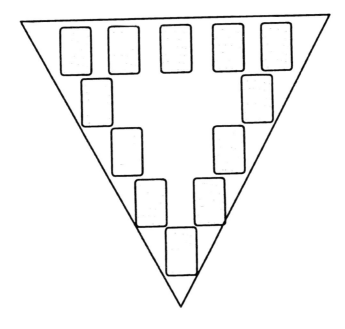

Again the system of this spread is quite simple. Although we have used the bodymind levels of mental, physical and emotional (the three biorhythmic curves) there is no reason why this method could not be used within the context of any tripartite system, for example:

Psychological Spread

unconscious - top line of triangle
Conscious - left hand side of triangle.
Ego - right hand side of triangle

(In this spread the information pertaining to the three major level in the individual psyche are exposed. Such information would be of great benefit if you wish to counsel someone or need more detailed information as to their state of mind before tackling a more 'mundane' problem.)

Examination Spread

Learning - top line of triangle
Recall - left hand side of triangle.
Paper - right hand side of triangle

(In this example, a student about to take an exam could take an opportunity to assess their own knowledge of the course work covered (learning), their memory and ability to apply that work (recall), and the nature of the paper and therefore to see if they are fully prepared. For instance, if it appears that the line of cards relating to the paper shows misfortune and frustration, and the cards, relating to the practical aspects of learning, show a mind clouded by facts and figures; then the student would be advised to go away and spend more time working on the practical section of their studies.)

Business Spread

Strengths/Weaknesses - top line of triangle.
Opportunities - left hand side of triangle
Threats - right hand side of triangle.

(In this context the spread can be used to deal with the management and development of a business or indeed any project. It is based upon the SWOT (an acronym for 'strength, weaknesses, opportunities, threats') system but in the spread is condensed The top line can show both strengths and therefore weaknesses in the organisation.)

The central cards in may be seen as the figure-heads or 'key cards' to each line. Essentially, they act as a sort of summing up, much as a lawyer will sum up a case before closing on a few words. By using a triangle, you can create a spread in which each line of enquiry relates to every other and the relationship (using the 'biorhythm' format above) between the mental & physical, the physical & emotional and emotional & mental are clarified. Try to find other ways in which this spread can be used.

The Fifteen Card Spread

This method provides a highly simplified form of a reading system which was constructed by Aleister Crowley (the full version is reprinted in the, sadly rare, publication of The Equinox Vol I No.8 or in the more commonly available Book of Thoth.) The cards are dealt thus:

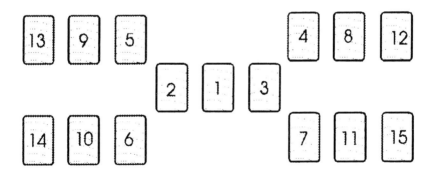

Card 1 - is the significator or, possibly, represents the most important person in the reading (this need not necessarily be the querant).

Cards 2 & 3 - represent the clients' situation, personality and immediate status.

Cards 13, 9, 5, 4, 8 and 12 - represent possible future developments. They may be two sides of the same possibility or the cards may be seen as describing the development of a future situation (running from most immediate, far left, to most distant, far right). If the cards on left and right describe opposing situations then the cards on the right may be taken as representing the direction events will take unless the querent chooses another course of action. The cards on the upper left describe alternative possibilities, should action be taken.

Cards 6, 10 & 14 - assist the client in understanding the situation by outlining psychological and environmental factors which can be changed, and the implications of doing so.

Cards 7, 11 & 15 - show forces which are operating beyond the querents' immediate control. These may include other personalities, physiological or environmental factors. From this information it may also be seen how the client could adapt to, and work with, these forces.

From your own knowledge you will be able to devise other spreads. If you have a knowledge of astrology (or intend to study this subject) then you could try the following spread.

Zodiac Spread

Place the cards in the form of a circle as indicated, from 1 to 12. You will then need to place a further ten cards (to represent the ten planets used in astrology; Sun, Moon, Mercury, Venus, Mars, Jupiter, Saturn, Uranus, Neptune & Pluto). These cards should be placed around the inside of the circle but according to your intuition (thus the following diagram is an example not a 'correct' method).

You should then interpret the fall of the inner ten cards in relation to the astrological functions of the 'houses', that is the twelve cards forming the circle. The aspects ruled by the houses are as follows:

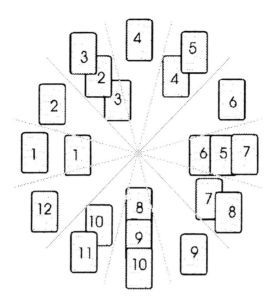

House 1 - The personality, in the true sense, as the 'persona' or mask which we display to others. This house is concerned with self-expression and self-image, thus the way the querent generally appears to others.

House 2 - personal resources, individual financial security (often in the sense of property of land). Also the immediate effects resulting from the persona adopted in house 1.

House 3 - personal expression and communication. This house described the relationship between the persona and the immediate environment. Short journeys and immediate relatives are also ruled by this house.

House 4 - domestic situation, psychological foundations of the individual and family (especially parents).

House 5 - family resources (often children), expressions of personal creative ability (often in an artistic sense). The individuals' romantic life in the sense that it shows the expression of that aspect which grows from the factors founded in the fourth house.

House 6 - employment, and general matters of health are held under the auspices of this house. Personal service to others and pets are also detailed here.

House 7 - others and their relationship with the individual (outlined in house 1) are important here. Business, marriage and other partnerships as well as persons antagonistic to the individual.

House 8 - the sexual nature of the individual is described here. This house governs all occult matters - from things 'magickal' through to unconscious desires. This house also indicates the individuals' ability to use things and people around them to assist in the transformation either of the self or of others. Matters legal and issues concerning death are also detailed here.

House 9 - kin folk (such as in-laws), religious and moral issues are covered here, as are long journeys, higher education and personal understanding and relationship to the dominant morality of the culture in which the individual lives.

House 10 - dominant characters in the individuals' life (parents, heroes or mentor), social implications of ones' employment or standing in the community - the 'public image' is displayed here.

House 11 - friends and associates are relevant to this house. The process by which the individuals' perspective becomes broadened, ideals and aspirations both social and ethical are described here.

House 12 - hidden factors (akin to those of the 8th house) are important here. This house deals with the individuals' ability to overcome entrenched patterns of behaviour and the ability to flow with and not against the natural current in the universe.

The ten cards will show you the most important factors in the individual at present (and past). You need not try to identify any one of the ten cards with a planetary force but, if you know something of astrology, then you may interested to trying it. Focus your attention on the houses which have a card 'within' them. Now, using your intuition, look at the cards, not as statements of what is or was but as statements about what is yet to be. You may wish to put out another series of ten cards, within the same circle (alternatively repeat the whole spread). This time, you are concerned with the changes depicted in the future.

With practice, this method can be extremely effective but a full knowledge of the houses is necessary (consult the bibliography for books on astrology which could help you here). The key to any reading, whether you choose to use a set spread or not, is in the relationship of the cards. If you find a spread which acts as a suitable vessel into which you can pour your intuition then all well and good - but don't let your own style become cramped by trying to make your intuitions fit in with any rigid method of using the tarot.

Naturally, you should record the results of all your experiments in your magickal diary. You may also wish to record the positioning in which cards appear in a given spread, for future reference. Try as many different methods as possible, reading for yourself, volunteers and actual clients. You will find from experimentation the spreads you are most comfortable with.

The more systems your unconscious has available to choose from the better. (Incidentally, if you have kept notes on the configurations formed when you have just 'thrown out' a series of cards you may find that you have already been using a documented spread structure.)

Meditation

Go to your quiet room and relax your bodymind complex. Imagine that you are sitting in the centre of an immense void of space; as you look around become aware of the presence of innumerable brilliant stars in the sky about you. Now understand that each star is a group of ideas, much like an individual tarot card. Consider that each star emits light which flows outward towards all of the other stars. Observe the infinite array of interrelationships between the stars in your night sky. Be aware that these are as numerous are the relationships within the tarot. This meditation is very difficult and you are unlikely either to be able to 'see' or 'feel' the interconnectedness of the stars at first. Repeat the exercise and, if you have done your background work on meditation properly, you should see just how profound an experience this meditation can provide.

- Breaking Away

This is the penultimate chapter which will examine your past progress, revise any previous work and deal with some of the implications of your learning. It will also deal with the issue of the tarots' place in many orthodox belief systems and the points at which the dominant culture/beliefs in Western industrialised society and the tarot part company.

Taking Your Self Out

By now you will have encountered a number of aspects of yourself which require analysis, understanding and integration into the self as a whole. One of the features of magick is that when quite ordinary, well-balanced people involve themselves with magickal issues, they suddenly find their world turned upside down. This is not an effect of any Satanic (or indeed Godly) force.

The majority of 'normal' people are full of repressed emotions, undirected thoughts, unresolved desires and fears. For many, being able to get up, go to work, and sleep at night are signs of being a well integrated person: yet repressed elements from the unconscious will always, eventually, assert themselves. Areas of the unconscious mind are locked off by the ego - contained rather like atomic waste. Yet even with the most solid container it is inevitable that the waste will seep out - magick accelerates this process, it is the equivalent of exerting an ever increasing, crushing pressure on the containment vessel created by the ego. How has this acceleration of experience occurred in your life?

Go through your magickal diary and look for any points where life seemed to 'shift up a gear'. What happened? How were the events precipitated? Are you still travelling at 'high gear' or have you had oscillating periods of activity and comparative calm?

Changing your Life

Try the following exercises. Some of them may seem obscure, even extreme, each one is designed to help you understand yourself better. To really use the tarot, in any context, you must understand the features of yourself.

Medicine Wheel

As you did with the pentacle exercise (in the last Spirit Chapter), draw out a large circle. Divide it up into a series of quadrants; e.g health, relationships, self- development, work, enjoyment.

Fill in each quadrant with written words, cuttings from magazines, drawings or any other media, the things you would like to see happening in your life in these areas. Hang the medicine wheel somewhere conspicuous in your dwelling place. See how the ideas which you have made manifest in your medicine wheel, realise themselves over the next six months.

Going Away

It is often important to have time just to 'be'. In our society we tend to think of such time as wasted but it is important for the health of your bodymind that you take the opportunity to spend time alone, with yourself and the environment (what used to be called time to 'get your head together'). The following exercises are not intended to be in any way ascetic in the sense of cutting yourself off from life, but are designed to clarify your perspective on things uncluttered by the daily rush of events.

Just Three Hours

Take three hours off. In that time, do not include travelling time, preparational time, even time to do any exercises. Go to a place which you love, preferably outdoors, and just relax.

Day of Rest

Many cultures who flourish in the present Western society and are able to maintain a sense of the 'inner nature' do so because they allow one day a week to obtain this 'bodymind space'. This space is preserved by ritual and custom which maintain the sanctity of that special time (e.g the Shabbat of the Jews). Try the following:

1) Be alone (from other humans) for a full 24 hours.

2) Allow your digestive system (both physical & mental) to relax by drinking only water and/or fruit juices.

3) Do not speak for 24 hours.

You can do these practices separately but it is best to combine them all, perhaps with a visit to a tranquil spot in the country.

Picture Yourself

Draw, or make five collages. Each one of yourself as;

1) A wise prophet.
2) A beggar.
3) A superhero.
4) A business tycoon.
5) A great artist.

How do you see yourself in these guises? How do you see others who are (or who you suppose to be) in these actual situations?

Death & Change

Whether you subscribe to any doctrine of post-mortem existence (from 'the life everlasting' to reincarnation), the thought of your own death and that of others must still be a very important, often painful issue. You will have seen by now that all things change and that death is certainly one of the most dramatic changes. The conscious apprehension of the reality of death takes years, but the understanding and integration of this process is essential to self development. Death cannot be viewed as an evil or final process. for whatever else it is, it is a natural process; a process which begins before conception and continues into the unknown.

Encounters with other people and with the inner levels of yourself will bring you face to face with the notion of death in all senses.

Dying Descriptions

Take two pages in your magickal record and write about your own death. Focus on any and all aspects of the process and let your language form from emotion and not reason. Repetition of this practice every six months will help to show you how your attitudes and feelings change.

Rebirth through sleep

The loss of consciousness upon falling asleep and subsequent awakening in the morning can be seen as a replay of the death/rebirth (death/resurrection or death/reincarnation - depending upon your belief) cycle.

Before you sleep, be aware that you are about to lose consciousness, to die a miniature death. Don't become concerned but remember that this is a natural function of change which is the vital precursor to rebirth. As you relax, prior to sleep imagine all your concerns drifting away with every breath you exhale. Consider too, that when you awake you will be reborn - a new being that has undergone rebirth experience. If your situation allows, re-affirm these statements by excluding electric light. Watch the sun set and then retire to bed. You will find (especially if you repeat this exercise, and leave your bedroom curtains open) that you awaken at sunrise. Go outside and greet the sun which is reborn each day, as you are, from the unconsciousness of sleep.

The Last Three Years

Go to your quiet room and relax your bodymind complex. Focus your attention on your breathing and then consider the following script;

Imagine that you have just been informed by your doctor that you have exactly three years to live. There will be no pain or disability in this time but there is no hope of a remission or cure either.

How would you feel? Would you be happy at the face of release from this troubled life? Would you immediately plan out your next three years, or would you rage against the injustice and horror of three short years?

Now rather than thinking about your possible anger or the possibility of life after death, start to work out how you wish to spend your last three years.

With whom would you like to spend your time? Where would you live? Would you work or study? What experiences would you like to have?

After imagining this script, relax again and then record your results and decisions in the fantasy, in your diary. What are the differences and similarities between your life now and the life that you would wish to experience in your last three years? Are there any elements that you would wish to incorporate from your fantasy into your present reality?

Taking Command of your Space

Take command of the way your living space is set up. Many of us end up living in cluttered environments surrounded by 'things' which have little benefit either as tools or accessories to the health of the bodymind complex.

Get rid of any 'clutter' you may have accumulated. Move furnishings if necessary and make your dwelling place a location in which you can feel invigorated and relaxed (just as your quiet room should be). Has your interest in tarot spawned any 'esoteric clutter' in the form of zodiac wall mirrors, ornamental renditions of the pyramids or a collection of 'sacred stones' by the sofa? Do these things actually help your self development, do you like them or are they possibly intended as a subliminal showmanship of your 'magickal wisdom'?

Do Something
This week do something that you have always wanted to do, no matter how seemingly small or unimportant it is.

Explaining Yourself
Go to your quiet room and select a card from your deck. Now explain yourself to the card, treat it as a living being (perhaps it will even answer you). The personality of this being is shown by the image depicted on its' surface. Just talk to the card, preferably aloud. Explain to it why you are doing the exercise, what you hope to learn, what you believe, what you have experienced. Keep an open mind and don't be afraid that this practice is foolish. Repeat this exercise once a week for as long as you like, selecting a new card at random. (A variation on this would be to pick a specific card and talk to it about a specific subject. E.g. Atu XIII about death, or The Ace of Disks about your material situation.)

Remembering
The aim of the exercise is to allow you a method of integrating past experiences in your life which may still be causing you problems. We all grow, at least in part, from our conscious experience and from which our memory is formed. Some memories can be limiting but even the harshest past can be turned into a rich compost from which you can grow anew. This exercise is best done with a close friend but can be adapted and used with a tape recorder, the written word or told to a tarot card (preferably an appropriate one) as in the exercise above.

Select an event in your life which is still very painful, one that repeatedly surfaces and constrains or confuses your participation in the now by chaining you to the then.

1. Relate the event as a sad story.
2. Tell the story for another persons' point of view.

3. Tell the story from the imagined perspective of an advanced alien observer or ancient, enlightened sage.

4. Tell the story as though it were a happy occurrence.

5. Tell the story as a situation comedy.

If you are telling the story to a friend they should be quiet, only interjecting to ask you to clarify a part of the story if necessary.

Now tell the story a sixth time in a way which 'empowers' or strengthens (rather than limits) you now. This may be a completely different version or an mixture of any of the first five relations of the tale.

Go to your quiet room and relax. Replay in your mind the whole event in a way that you would have wanted it to be. Don't be concerned that this way is not 'the truth'. As you have seen truth is relative, and in magick maximum convenience is our canon of truth. So if the new story of re-memory helps empower you then that is the important thing.

It may take some time to rearrange your memories in a way which is conducive to your development but it is certainly worth doing.

Beyond Belief

The use of the tarot is not limited by belief. However, it must be said that there are points at which magick and many belief systems reach an impasse. (There are of course some limiting religious structures which forbid totally the use of divination; particularly in cults designed to inhibit any form of self discipline and discovery. One might believe (and we are not saying that this belief for the believer is 'untrue') that Jesus Christ is the Messiah who died for our sins and was resurrected in the flesh, encountering other dying figures, such as Atu XII 'The Hanged Man' need not be a problem, but deities from Pagan cultures could be! The tarot speaks of a cyclical, ever changing, flow of energies - how can this be reconciled with Christ's physical resurrection in the same flesh? Perhaps more importantly, the Tarot, and all forms of occultism suggest that self development is to be found through the self not through any guru, messiah, master or teacher.

This is, arguably, the most difficult proposition for orthodox religion to handle. Orthodoxy in anything implies that there is an absolute standard by which all people should measure their actions. Yet in magick there is no definite way, in fact all of occultism is about giving the individual keys to unlock the doors themselves. There is also no 'truth absolute' which makes a mockery of orthodoxy which must, to hold credence, claim to be 'the way, the truth, the light.'

As you study the tarot, you will inevitably find that beliefs you have held for some considerable time, are at odds with your studies, ideas or results. There is no point in glossing over these differences - they do exist. What you must do is either learn to enlarge your belief or else put aside your studies (though the questions will still remain).

It is essential that you recognise the possibility of there being more than one way of viewing the universe, and that your own belief needs not be static to remain true. The only thing you will, inevitably, have to give up is reliance on orthodoxy - in society, in religion, in education, in yourself. This is not the same as giving up structure, for organisation is vital to all beings. It means taking the notion of the 'True Will' to heart (see last Spirit chapter). Use all methods at your disposal to find your own knowledge, power and perception to evolve your own belief structures. Initially, it is important to have a foundation to build on. One cannot paint surrealist landscapes without a knowledge of the traditional manner of rendering a landscape painting. However once the core techniques are fully mastered there are, quite literally, no limits.

The principles of the magickal universe are simple but in application are often seen as clouded and complex. Consider the following statements (especially number VII in relation to the issues of orthodoxy and belief systems).

I) 'As above, so below' - the Whole is encoded within each of its constituents - every part contains the whole as microcosm and macrocosm.

II) The Whole is interconnected, every aspect of the universe is intimately related to every other.

III) The Whole is self-organising, and the same essential principles of organisation govern the evolution of all forms.

IV) By means of trained Will, beings may effect change at various levels of organisation.

V) Change is the only universal constant.

VI) The Whole is more than merely the sum of its' parts.

VII) Our beliefs define the limits of what we may consciously experience.

VIII) The 'everyday reality' which we experience is only one fraction of the total of existence. By changing our level of awareness we can directly perceive other aspects of reality.

IX) Magickal ability is engendered through this process in the form of an inward, transformative journey.

Any belief should act like a spring board from which new experiences, knowledge, understanding and wisdom may evolve. Orthodoxy and rigidity in personal belief creates mental' dead wood' which limits the experience of the conscious mind. Consciously formed belief cannot hold sway over what the unconscious knows. The unconscious mind is naturally formed from universal principles such as those outlined above. Many of the problems in the individual and humanity as a whole, occur when the dominant belief of the conscious mind and the knowledge of the unconscious (or 'natural law') are at odds. Puritanism was a consciously formulated belief that designated sex as wrong, sinful, evil, etc.. This belief was formulated at an abstract level and was at odds with the unconscious, natural fact that sexuality is a vital element in human nature. As a result of this irreconcilable situation, neuroses, sexual guilt, abuse, sadness and the eventual decline in the belief occurred.

While the use of the tarot may be an acceptable part of many faiths you will need to consider how the changes in you and your faith can co-exist, if at all.

Another vital consideration is the nature of belief and faith itself. The eminent psychologist and magickian Carl Gustav Jung was once asked 'do your believe in God?'. His reply was 'I do not believe, I know.' Belief necessitates faith and faith itself does not fit well with magick. We all entertain a simple set of beliefs for the purposes of conscious convenience. We believe that the sun will rise tomorrow - we don't know for certain but our belief is based on past experience, knowledge of astronomy and unconscious realisation. In this example, belief is more of a hypothesis than a faith. As any scientist will tell you a hypothesis is a model of the universe - it may not be 'true' (in the absolute sense) but it may be applied as if it were. The second law of thermodynamics of physics states that hot things tend to get colder. This hypothesis can be applied as an inviolable fact in the smelting of metals or the cooling of cups of coffee. However this 'law' is subject to change and revision. This particular hypothesis does not work, as physicists have discovered, at the sub-atomic level. In other words all rules apply except when they don't!

Try the following to put your own beliefs in perspective.

Listing Belief

In your magickal record, list out six beliefs which you held as a child, six things you believe now, six things you might believe and six things you could not (at this point in your life) accept. Analyse why you believe, no longer believe or could not believe in these statements. How has your own self development changed your belief?

Explanations

Imagine a conversation between yourself and another. The person could be the woman next door, Plato, Leonardo da Vinci, Queen Elizabeth or Mussolini. How would you explain the core of your own worldview? Explain your personal criteria for either believing or not believing any statement.

Meditation on Faith

Consider the central beliefs of as many different religions, philosophies and methods of self development as possible. Research any you are not familiar with. Contrast orthodox religious movements, such as Judaism and Islam with self- development methods, such as Taoism and Thelema. Consider two opposing philosophical structures from Nihilism to Hedonism. At what points do these systems intersect? Where are they opposed? Where do they exhibit different aspects of the same thing?

- # The Tarot on Fire

The element of fire is the most energetic and therefore the least stable of the elements. It is the one most associated with the nature of the True Will because fire is about activity, going, moving, change in its most rapid and dramatic sense. As you have seen all the elements contain both active and passive aspects, in fire, this duality is manifested as fire which consumes, destroys and obliterates and fire which focuses, directs and constrains. To see these twin, complimentary aspects of fire, consider the flame which burns wood to fine ash, reducing the once living form to its basic constituents which in turn become reabsorbed into the framework of other trees. On the other hand, fire may be seen as a laser beam, a fine, carefully focused beam of light which, by its very intensity, can cut solid objects in two.

At a psychological level the fire element is concerned with the most fundamental action/reaction systems. The association of fire with 'passions' such as sexuality, anger, courage & fear reflect this.

The three elements of earth, water and air are unified by the vital, active 'inner nature' (fire) of the individual and are unified to become spirit. Before examining the ways in which the tarot may be used within the context of ritual, here are some exercises intended to put you in tune with the fiery level of the universe, both inner and outer.

Facing the Cards

Select three cards, this may be done at random or deliberately. One card represents you, one an important person in your life (mother, partner, brother or other relation), and one an impersonal force (e.g death, time, love, hunger etc.). Go to your quiet room and place the first card in front of you - begin to talk to it. You will, undoubtedly, feel silly to start with but once you get over your shyness you will find that words come thick and fast. Get angry with the card, express all your pent up rage at whatever it stands for. Demonstrate your love, affection any other emotion you feel towards it, verbally.

Write down your results afterwards (you may wish to tape record what you say to each card - in the heat of the moment you may use phrases which are worthy of later analysis).

Child Watching

Children are tremendously fiery creatures. If you are a parent or guardian then you will know this from experience. Even if you are not a parent you can learn much from observing children; watch them play with other children - quietly take an interest (circumstances permitting, an active interest) in the way children act. Watch the way they can instantly shift moods from extreme sadness and depression to elated joy. Young children have not yet developed a conscious relationship with the other three elements (earth/body, water/emotions, air/intellect) and are more spontaneous and impetuous than adults.

Discipline

Fire is also the element of discipline, that is the self regulated structuralisation which we have talked about in this book.

Look back at your diary and see just how disciplined you have been in your practices.

Try the following exercise in self discipline:

Set out walking wherever you are. See how far you can walk before you begin to feel bored, when you find this barrier, cross through it and continue walking. Don't put any major stress on your physical organism but be prepared to press yourself.

Being Positive

The following exercises are concerned with the active, positive aspects of fire.

Positive Moving

Record each time in the day when your physical movement was not positive and certain, e.g hesitation before knocking on the bosses door, pacing the floor nervously, accidentally spilling a cup of coffee. After a day or so spent just becoming aware of your body movement, spend the following seven days moving positively. Begin by consciously correcting your movement - if you are in the habit of walking with short paces, head bowed, make an effort to walk with wider, more positive steps and with your head raised. After a while you should see how an initially consciously adopted positive movement will seem perfectly natural. Record how you feel after your week's practice and whether other people reacted differently to you.

146

Burning Thought Off at the Root

This exercise is a type of meditation. Go to your quiet room and relax your bodymind complex. Breathe deeply and let any undirected thoughts come and go as they will. When you feel ready begin to consciously prevent unbidden thoughts arising. You could incorporate a visualisation/imagination construct here:- 'seeing' each thought, as it arises, as a sphere of energy which you literally vaporise with your will. Your aim is to capture each undesired intrusion into your consciousness, to give it a form (thus, in a sense, freezing it, and preventing the emerging thought from becoming a train of thought) and then destroying it. Try this exercise, every other day, for two weeks. Eventually you should find that you are becoming vigilant over your consciousness, remaining 'at the centre' as it were. (Incidentally this exercise is one of the origins of the horror stories about magickians sacrificing babies, the children that the magickian sought to slay were not physical offspring but rather 'thoughts slain err they could arise into consciousness'.)

Reclaiming Activities

Over the course of a week reclaim activities into your control which you would normally give to others. For instance, start making your own bread (vigorously kneading the dough is a great way of releasing tension). If you use the bus be the first one to ring the bell for your stop, don't rely on others. Take charge of your own life.

Corresponding Clothes

Using the system of correspondences mentioned in the last Hexagram chapter, experiment with using them in everyday life. One way to do this is to wear clothes of colours which correspond to the appropriate day of the week.

Day	Planetary Ruler	Colour
Sunday	Sun	Yellow
Monday	Moon	Violet
Tuesday	Mars	Red
Wednesday	Mercury	Orange
Thursday	Jupiter	Blue
Friday	Venus	Green
Saturday	Saturn	Indigo

Using these colours you could wear a red tie on Tuesday or a green dress on Friday. Try wearing the appropriate colours of each planet on each day in a week. Record how you felt on each day. Did wearing the colours of the Sun on Sunday make you feel happy and 'sunny'? Did people react differently to you during this week? You could also adapt this exercise to other media; for instance wearing appropriate perfumes such as frankincense oil on Sunday, red sandalwood on Friday. Alternatively you could use appropriate jewellery such as a moonstone brooch on Monday. Combine these activities, record and analyse your results.

Using Ritual

Defining ritual is almost impossible, however the basic functions of ritual may be see as a three fold system.

Communication within the levels of self.

Communication with other entities (i.e animals, plants, people).

Communication with place (the bioregion and planet as whole).

Ritual is communication (the word communication is related to communion which is an important aspect of ritual), the linking together of different, often opposing, systems, levels, ideas, people and ecosystems.

Within the context of the tarot, as a means of self exploration, you will be primarily concerned with the first form of communication - between your conscious mind and other levels in yourself. As you practice you will soon see that the microcosm/macrocosm paradox asserts itself again, and that the 'self' you are exploring is, in fact, the whole universe.

Each card in the deck may be seen as an archetype or aspect of yourself and, by ritual, your conscious mind may be aligned with these aspects. The process is rather akin to setting up an electric circuit so that power flows freely through all sections of the system.

The difficulty and, paradoxically the great benefit of ritual, is that it is performed at the deepest (or 'highest') levels of the self and at the most basic, physical level. Ritual integrates the elemental processes in unison - producing spirit.

The Performance of Ritual

Ritual takes many forms; from the complex ceremonies of the Thelemic Gnostic mass, to the superficially simple rites of the Native American Shaman.

The most important item you will require for ritual work is your trained bodymind complex. To accomplish the full integration of the elements you will need to conduct your rituals on the physical plane as well as all the other levels of reality. For all the following rituals, you will need your tarot deck, your quiet room (or an outdoor location in which you can work without disturbance). We would also advise you to make or purchase a number of items, these are:

The Altar - the altar is used as the focal point for your ritual. It could consist of a small table, chest or tree stump. The only important factor is that it should provide a flat surface on which you can rest your equipment.

The Pentacle - the pentacle is the Disk in the tarot and represents the element of Earth. This could be a disk of copper, a section cut from a tree trunk, or a flat circular stone. If you can make this, and your other, 'magickal weapons' then so much the better, if this is not possible, check out your nearest antique/junk shop or Esoteric store which may be able to provide you with paraphernalia.

The Chalice - this weapon is related to the element of water and the suit of Cups. A silver chalice (silver being the metal corresponding to the Moon) is the traditional object but there is no reason why a drinking horn, clay cup or gourd bowl could not be used.

The Dagger - the air element and the suit of Swords are made physical in this weapon. The dagger is usually a knife with a double edged blade.

The Wand - Fire and the suit of Wands are related to this weapon. It is usually constructed of a length of wood or metal, about the length of your forearm. Details of its manufacture should be determined by you and not what any 'books on magick' say.

You may wish to consecrate these objects, especially if they are bought and not made by you. To do this simply repeat the process of handling them and keeping them within your aura as you did with your cards (consult the texts of magick in the bibliography to help in this respect).

In addition to these tools you will need a censer or vessel in which you can burn incense. Joss sticks, while useful for meditation, are not particularly effective in ritual magick. Gums, resins and aromatic woods burnt on charcoal emit a far more enveloping scent and it is easier to make-up or obtain incenses which are made from materials which correctly correspond to the force you wish to work with. You will also require candles which serve to mark particular points of focus in the ritual and to give you light to work by (most people find that ritual work is best conducted at night).

In one sense, the aim of all these objects is to assist in focusing your bodymind complex to the work in hand. They also serve to 'concretise' the ritual so that, unlike using a pathworking, the experience takes place as much on the physical level as it does on the astral plane. We have kept the dramatic and verbose elements, in the following rites, down to the minimum. Ritual should be inspirational, so, if you play a musical instrument then use that, if you find poetry awakens your spirit use that.

It is here that the system of correspondences comes into its own. As with constructing a pathworking using correctly corresponding images, ideas, scents, symbols etc., so ritual uses the same 'conceptual chains' to link-up, or communicate between, various levels of the self. This is why the magickal weapons spoken of above relate to the same four-fold elemental structure. They are the physical expression of the elemental qualities in the form of the most basic human tools; a platter to eat from (or stone to build with), a vessel to drink from, a blade to cut with, and a stick or staff to walk with.

The following rituals are examples. Again study them, experiment with them and then, once you fully understand their construction, develop your own methods:-

Archetypal Experience Ritual

Always perform rituals for a reason. Even the simplest rite conducted properly will have long term consequences, just as a pathworking will. The aim of both methods is to put your conscious mind into alignment with a given archetypal force, as expressed through the tarot. Thus the force, bridges the division between consciousness and your unconsciousness - integrating each level of the Self (taken as a whole) with every other.

You will find some archetypal forces are simple to work with, while the experience of others will be like coming face-to-face with all 'horrors' from the mental abyss. In any case, it is important that you begin the life-long process of opening up the channels of communication between these various levels or aspects of yourself.

The following ritual uses the Queen of Disks as the archetype in question. By understanding correspondences it will be easy for you to adapt the format of the rite to open up a communication with any of the other 77 archetypes in the tarot. This ritual may look deceptively simple but if your training in organised imagination and your bodymind exercises have been thorough, it will be effective.

Preparation

Go to the location of the ritual (your temple). If the altar is moveable it should be placed in the appropriate quarter (The Queen of Disks, being an Earth card, the corresponding direction the North in most European countries). If you are able, cover the altar with a cloth, preferably of an earthy colour. Place two candles on the altar as shown. It is preferable if the colour of the candles correspond correctly to the force concerned.

Place a further four candles at each point in your temple, one at each cardinal point. (The 'traditional' colours for these candles are: East, yellow - South, red - West, blue and North green or brown.) In doing this you will have formed a circle. The circle represents the circumference of your own auric 'egg', and is the symbol for infinity or the womb.

Light a suitable earth incense (formulated by making use of Crowley's' 777 or a good incense stockist) and the candles. Place your pentacle, dagger, wand and chalice (filled with water, fruit juice or red wine) on the altar. The drink in the chalice will be used later at the 'sacramental' stage of the rite. Ideally red wine should be used as this symbolises blood/life (see Seeds of Magick). You will also need to place a morsel of bread on your pentacle.

Place your tarot deck on the altar.

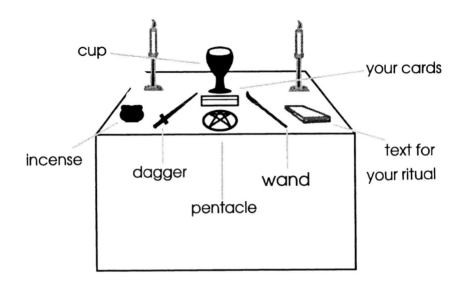

cup

your cards

incense

text for
your ritual

dagger

wand

pentacle

Stage 1. Relaxation. Take a few moments to relax your bodymind. Use the breathing methods taught earlier. Sit in the centre of your temple and prepare yourself. (Don't worry about feeling nervous, a spattering of this anticipation will actually enhance the ritual.)

Stage 2. Take your deck from the altar and select the Queen of Disks card from it. As you do so, become aware that this is the aspect of yourself (which, in the whole sense, is the sum of the cards in the deck) that you are going to concentrate on. Place the Queen of Disks on the altar so that it stands upright. Replace the remainder of the deck on the altar.

Stage 3. Take the wand from your altar and stand in the centre of your temple. Point the wand outward and turn, describing a circle around you. As you do this, become aware of, the auric field surrounding you and forming the boundary in which the rite will occur. You may wish to visualise a sphere of light enfolding your temple as you do so. Replace the wand on the altar.

Stage 4. Use the Cross of Powers centring rite or another form of your own devising. Affirm in this way that your bodymind complex encompasses all things - in a sense, you are god (having all the elements of the universe within you), in the centre of your circle (a microcosmic rendition of the whole universe).

Stage 5. Stand before your altar and focus your attention on the Queen of Disks card. Use a poem, a chant or dance to invoke (that is, 'draw down') the energy of this card. The following invocation is based on the symbolism of the Queen of Disks archetype and the imagery in the Thoth tarot deck.

"Queen of Disks.
You who are the force of the fertilising waters,
That bathe the earth and bring forth life.
I call on your power.
Crowned with the horns of majesty.
Enthroned in the mountain crag,
Earth growing organic as a crystal in the heart of me!
I draw your power down into this my temple."

If you are using words to do this section of the rite you may find many things occurring. You may find yourself supplanting new words (incidentally these lines are best memorised but may be read from this book or a script), or notice an odd intonation creeping into your voice. In any event, remember that the words, chant or music is only a means to an end and any spontaneous adaptation is all to the good.

Stage 6. Remove your wand from the altar and direct it at the image of the Queen of Disks. Draw with the wand an invoking Earth pentagram thus:

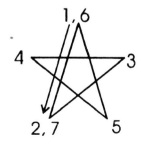

Imagine the pentagram forming as your move your arm, alternatively visualise each line as a flaming trail, coloured appropriately. This serves to provide a 'window' through which the force can flow from your unconscious into your conscious awareness. (The drawing of pentagrams, which is an important part of Western ritual magick, may be seen as another way of focusing your attention). Alternatively an intrinsic 'mystical' power may be thought of as residing in the process itself. In practice, a mixture of these attitudes is best, while in the ritual all that is important is that you know it will work. The result is the most important thing and the process which arrives at the result secondary. The 'truth' of how the pentagram works in ritual is of no real importance. Open yourself out and allow the force of the Queen of Disks to flow into you. Spend some time in this state.

Stage 7 - when you feel ready remove the chalice from the altar and hold it up in both hands. Focus your attention on the Queen of Disks. Say, and more importantly become aware of, the following.

"Queen of Disks,
Drain your power into this wine,
that I may partake of your essence.
Fill this liquid with your life,
which is my life,
As your rivers fertilise the earth,
which is my body."

Drink from the chalice and replace it on the altar. Stage 8 - Repeat this process with the pentacle, holding it up with the bread upon it say:

"Queen of Disks, Infuse your power within this bread,
that I may partake of your essence.
Suffuse this food with your life,
Which is my life,
As your earth endures and grows,
so do I."

Eat a little of the bread and replace the pentacle on the altar.

Stage 9 - Spend a while in your temple just being. Don't try to analyse at this point, the time for that is later. If you want to meditate, eat and drink, listen to music, or even run around screaming, do so! Don't try to rationalise anything until afterwards.

Stage 10 - Clear up. When you feel ready, repeat the focusing exercise you used in stage 4. Clear up your temple (extinguish your candles, incense etc.) and retire to bed. Keep a special note of any dreams you have. You may find that the effects of the ritual may not be felt until some days afterwards, there is often an 'incubation' period prior to major changes as a result of the rite. There is no need to 'banish' the circle in this instance (unlike certain magickal rites in which the energy generated must be dispersed to prevent any lingering around the site of the work).

Elemental Centre Ritual

The aim of this ritual is harmonise the forces of the elements within you.

Preparation: Set your altar up in your quiet room or secluded outdoor location. Upon it should stand the following items; two candles (preferably coloured black on the left - yin, and white on the right - yang), incense (suitable for the four elements), dagger, chalice, dagger, wand and tarot deck. Your cards should be sorted, prior to the rite, into the following order, so that dealt from the top they fall:

Ten of Swords, Ten of Wands, Ten of Cups, Ten of Disks,
Nine of Swords, Nine of Wands, Nine of Cups, Nine of Disks, and so forth until;
Ace of Swords, Ace of Wands, Ace of Cups, Ace of Disks.
Knight of Swords, Knight of Wands, Knight of Cups, Knight of Disks,
Queen of Swords, Queen of Wands, Queen of Cups, Queen of Disks, and so on for the Prince & Princess cards, then;
Atu I, Atu XI, Atu II, Atu III, Atu IV, Atu XIV, Atu VII, Atu V, Atu VI, Atu XV, Atu XII, Atu VIII, Atu X, Atu XIX, Atu XIII, Atu IX, Atu XVI, Atu XX, Atu XVIII, Atu XVII, Atu O & Atu XXI.

Organising the deck into this order will allow you to position them around your circle, as part of the rite, without fumbling through the whole pack. You will require bread and wine for this ritual.

Stage 1 - Light your incense and candles. Sit for a while and relax.

Stage 2 - As with the ritual above 'cast' the circle using your wand.

Stage 3 - As you are going to work with the elemental energies you will need to consecrate your temple to each of these powers.

Take the chalice from the altar and go to stand in the Eastern quarter of your circle. Raise the chalice and sprinkle a few drops from it onto the earth with your fingers. Moving clockwise (following the direction that the sun moves in the Northern hemisphere) around the perimeter of your circle, stop at the South and repeat the process, thence to the West and North. Complete the circle by returning to the East and replace the chalice on the altar. The liquid in the chalice (which, ideally, should be salted water) represents the element of water - use whatever visualisation, or imaginative method you need to make this process come alive. Merely carrying a cup in circles round a room will not do anything unless you have Organised Imagination and Will to turn the 'play acting' of ritual into real experience. (It is not usually considered necessary to consecrate the temple in the earth element as it is already made of earth energy (matter).

Repeat this circumambulation with the incense burner for air - holding it aloft at each quarter, and with one of the altar candles, again lifting it in 'salute' at the cardinal directions.

Stage 4 - Take the dagger from the altar and move (always clockwise) to the Eastern point of the circle. Draw the invoking pentagram of Air with the blade using your imagination to call the elemental force of Air through the 'window area' or the pentagram. Once you have done this, place the dagger on the ground in the Eastern quarter.

Repeat this process with the wand, drawing the invoking Fire pentagram and leaving the weapon in the South.

Again with the chalice and pentacle, go to each appropriate quarter; draw the correct pentagram (for these two weapons you will need to put them down first and then draw the pentagram with your hands clasped together, forefingers extended).

Invoking

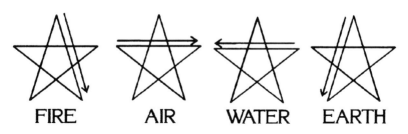

FIRE   AIR   WATER   EARTH

Stage 5 - Pick up your cards from the altar and go to stand in the centre of the circle. Say, and more importantly become aware of, the following:

"I am a Star,
I am enfolded in Infinite Space,
I am at the core of all that is,
I am everywhere,
I am the centre.
Now I draw the forces of the universe about me,
Dancing in their Veil,
Of creation and destruction,
Of eternal change."

Stage 6 - Circle the perimeter of your circle, clockwise, carrying the deck in your hands. Set down the first card in the East (which will be the Ten of Swords), the next in the South (Ten of Wands) and so on. You may lay the cards out just as you wish, in lines moving into the centre of the circle from the Ten on the perimeter to Ace, closer in. This method, if you have the space, is best as it causes you to make ever decreasing circumnambulations - rather like dancing an ancient maze into the depths of your psyche. Alternatively, you could lay the cards out in the form of a triangle with its' apex pointing toward the centre of the circle. Circle around, imagine that you are getting deeper and deeper into the nature of the four elements.

As you do this you might want to repeat a poem, use pre-recorded music, or chant. If you wish to chant we suggest the following mantras:

Aum - also written 'Om'. This is the 'seed sound' of the universe. It pronounced by breathing forcibly from the back of the throat and slowly closing the mouth producing a resonant, humming sound.

IAO - we have already dealt with the symbolism of this mantra (in the form of a magickal formula - see page XXX). It is pronounced in one breath 'ee-ah-oh', rhythmically rather like the 'yo-heaveho' of sailors.

A ka dua
Tuf ur biu
Bi aa chefu
Dudu ner af an nuteru

This mantra is from the ancient Egyptian language. It's use was first suggested by Aleister Crowley who transcribed it from an Egyptian artifact known as the 'Stele of Revealing'. Crowley's' translation runs:

Unity uttermost showed!
I adore the might of Thy breath,
Supreme & terrible God,
Who makest the Gods and Death
To Tremble before Thee:- I, I adore thee!

The letters are pronounced as they stand and chanted in the following fashion:

158

Stage 7 - Once you have put down the Ace cards you should continue your circumnambulations and place the Court cards:

East	South	West	North
Knight of Swords	Knight of Wands	Knight of Cups	Knight of Disks
Queen of Swords	Queen of Wands	Queen of Cups	Queen of Disks

- and so forth for the Prince & Princess cards.

Stage 8 - By now you should really be aware of the elemental forces converging and becoming increasingly focused on the centre of your circle. Continue to circle but this time place the first Major Arcana card in the South-East and round the circle thus:

South East	South West	North West	North East
Atu I	Atu XI	Atu II	Atu III
Atu IV	Atu XIV	Atu VII	Atu V
Atu VI	Atu XV	Atu XII	Atu VIII
Atu X	Atu XIX	Atu XIII	Atu IX
Atu XVI	Atu XX	Atu XVIII	Atu XVII

As you do this become aware of the connecting principle of the Major Arcana (connecting the increasingly focused elemental forces - just as the paths connect the spheres in the Qabalah).

Stage 9 - After placing the last card (i.e Atu XVII 'The Star', in the North East) go and stand in the centre of the circle. Face the altar and place Atu 0 'The Fool', and Atu XXI 'The Universe' on the ground, in front of you, on the left and right respectively. Feel the whole energy of the tarot, and therefore the whole universe (both micro and macrocosm) meeting within you. Say:

"As the Fool I began,
The child of the breath of Spirit.
Through the four elements I have travelled,
And become the Universe.
I am a Star,
And my light connects me to every part of the Cosmos.

I am One,
I am None,
I am All."

Stage 10 - When you are quite ready, reverse your steps and pick up the cards. Do this in silence. Drink a little of the wine and eat some of the bread - being aware that these things are suffused by elemental force (the bread is earth, the wine - water, the incense smoke - air and the candle light - fire).

Place the deck on the altar, extinguish the candles and incense and allow the circle to fade of its' own accord. You may wish to sleep after this, again keep a careful record of any dreams. The best time to perform this ritual is just before dawn. At the very least, you should make an effort to greet the rising sun, reaffirming the indivisible identity of spirit and matter.

Hanged Man Rite

The following ritual is designed to precipitate an initiatory experience which will allow you to access, previously hidden areas in your micro/macrocosm. We must stress that initiation is not an event but a process. As an ongoing situation, this rite will help accelerate this process. Having said this you should be warned that a ritual of this type can have far reaching consequences. Self understanding is often precipitated by events such as changes in ones' job & changes in relationships and often provokes a dramatic 'Apophis Phase' in the individual.

The symbolism of the Hanged Man, who is mythologically Osiris, Tammuz, Christ, Odin and many others, represents a descent into the primeval waters and period of silence (gestation). The ever changing forces in the universe seek to fill the 'vacuum' or stasis which this rite creates, thereby pushing the magickian into a new phase of accelerated change.

Preparation: As before, you will need to set up candles at each quarter, and appropriate incense. You should have your magickal weapons, wine, bread and your tarot placed upon the altar. If possible a suitably coloured altar cloth should be used (use your knowledge of correspondences here).

There should be four candles, one at each of the sub-cardinal points in the circle, and a single candle on the altar: (Incidentally the 'traditional colours for the sub-quarter candles are: SE - orange, SW - purple, NW - indigo & NE - black.)

Stage 1 - begin by casting your circle as given above.

Stage 2 - repeat the Cross of Powers exercise, or a similar method of focusing your bodymind.

Stage 3 - consecrate the circle using liquid, incense, and candle light as given above.

Stage 4 - take your tarot deck from the altar, which has already been sorted out. Circumambulate the circle from the East anti-clockwise (symbolically drawing up into yourself, following the direction that a newly fertilised ovum rotates in the womb). Place the following eight cards down on the perimeter of your circle:

East	**North-East**	**North**	**North-West**
Atu XX	Atu IX	Atu XVIII	Atu XIII

West	**South-West**	**South**	**South-East**
Atu XII	Atu XIV	Atu III	Atu 0

As you place each card down make a mental (or, if you wish, verbal) affirmation of your commitment to change, to initiation and to your True Will.

Stage 5 - return to face your altar and pick up the dagger. Holding it before you, make one circumambulation round the circle and place it in the East in front of the tarot card. Repeat this process with the wand, chalice and then pentacle (placing each weapon in its respective quarter). Each time make a full circle round the temple and, as you do so, imagine that you are drawing yourself inward.

Stage 6 - take the candle from the altar and move to the East (the place of the suns' 'birth'). Holding the light before you, move around the perimeter of the circle, until you are at the Western point. Move forward and place the candle in the centre of the circle and move back to the West.

Be aware of the fact that, though you would cast yourself into 'the darkness', there is an inner light that exists therein and that its' brightness is a function of, and not a rage against ,'the darkness' (i.e. depths of the unconscious).

Stage 7 - Moving from your position in the West, circle slowly and silently around the circle, again anti-clockwise. As you reach each of the candles in the sub-quarters snuff, or blow it out. Be aware of the encroaching darkness which resembles the darkness of the womb which you must enter to be re-born.

Stage 8 - Return to your position in the West. Either stand or sit facing the light in the centre of the circle. Close your eyes and become aware of your own breathing. You may find it helpful to curl up into a foetal position (don't worry in this instance if your spine is curved over). Don't analyse, think, imagine - just let it happen. Eventually you will feel the time is right to move, it may be a struggle physically or emotionally to do so, if you have problems, force your eyes open and look at the single flame which still burns in the darkness of your temple.

Stage 9 - move to the centre of the circle and raise the candle above you, if you wish to say anything do so - you may well find words (or even laughter or tears) spontaneously burst forth from you. Move clock-wise to the South East and re-light the candle from the one you are carrying. Take a moment to consider the card in this part of the circle. Move, to the South and put your candle down. Take up the wand and just hold it in your hands for a moment. Then continue round the circle, re-lighting the candles at the sub-quarters, drink some wine in the West, eat a little bread in the North. When you reach the East, take up the dagger and with it draw the symbol of the Unicursal Hexagram. This symbolises the active energy of the universe in total (the hexagram is symbol of the macrocosm, while the pentagram represents the microcosm).

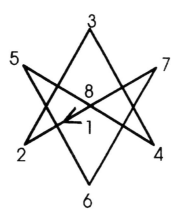

Stage 10 - as before, close the temple.

There are many ways of using the tarot for ritual and the best way to learn is not by studying this, or any other book, but by experience. With your past months of training you should be able, after a little practice, to invent your own methods and to combine the physical mechanics of ritual with the techniques of bodymind discipline, organised imagination, correspondences and a sense of humour.

Record all the details of your rites after you have done them. As with dreams, events which seem dramatic at the time soon slip into the unconscious mind.

☆ Time, Tide & Tarot

A problem which you may have encountered by now is in ascertaining, by divination, the timing of events. Consciously, we see time as a one way flow of events from 'yesterday', through 'now' to 'tomorrow'. Your intuition will usually only offer that an event may occur 'soon' or 'not for some time yet'. Naturally the client is likely to ask 'well just how long is 'some time'?'' To overcome this problem there are a number of systems available to you.

Key Time Scales

There is a system of ascribing a time factor to every one of the 78 cards in the Tarot. This method again presumes that cards have isolated meanings rather than meaning in relation to others. It also tends towards suggesting that a list structure is likely to be more valid than your own intuition. However, this method can provide some interesting and accurate results and so we have included it and would suggest that you experiment to see whether it works for you.

Atu 0 - This indicates that the event is either already upon the individual or possibly, that by their own unconscious action, the predicted event will be annulled.

Atu I - the next quarter of the moon will see the event come to pass (therefore, if you are reading, two days after the full moon, the event will occur in about five days time when the moon enters the third quarter).

Atu II - by or on the next new moon. (N.B. in magickal jargon 'new moon' refers to the first visible crescent of the moon. Astronomical new moon, usually given in diaries, refers to the time the moon is 'dark' or invisible in the sky. The first visible manifestation of the new moon is approximately three days after this.).

Atu III - first indications of the event in twenty eight days (about the length of one lunar cycle). The full manifestation of the event will not be for three months.

Atu IV - after one full lunar month (i.e if you are reading on the first day of the full moon, the event will not occur until the next full moon - around 28 days hence).

Atu V - six days hence.
Atu VI - within seven days.
Atu VII - within eight days.
Atu VIII - on the seventh day hence.

Atu IX - When the moon enters her last phase (i.e the next Third Quarter).

Atu X - ten days hence

Atu XI - within eleven days (the first manifestations are often felt on day seven).

Atu XII - on the ninth or twelfth day.

Atu XIII - there will be an unknown factor at work which will change the course of the event predicted or thwart it. Otherwise within thirteen days.

Atu XIV - within fourteen days

Atu XV - within fifteen days or until the next dark moon (astronomical 'new moon'), whichever is nearest.

Atu XVI - depending on the event in question this can mean that the event will occur immediately, within seven or sixteen days. In any case the event will be sudden and unexpected.

Atu XVII - seventeen days.

Atu XVIII - by the next full moon.

Atu XIX - a foreshadowing of the event will occur within the next 30 days but the full accomplishment of the event will not be until a year has elapsed.

Atu XX - within twenty one days (usually on the 20th day).

Atu XXI - one full lunar month. Ace of Wands - within one day, or at most one week.

From Two of Wands to Seven of Wands - the same number of days after the reading as the Wands on the card selected (thus Five of Wands - five days etc.).

Eight of Wands - swift news, perhaps a letter or telephone call hastens the matter which will occur within thirty days.

Nine of Wands - within twenty days.
Ten of Wands - within nineteen days.
Knight of Wands - within fifteen days.
Queen of Wands - within sixteen days.
Prince of Wands - within seventeen days.
Princess of Wands - within nineteen days.

Ace of Cups - one week or one month.

Two of Cups - two weeks or two months.

Three of Cups - there will be a speedy conclusion of events within one lunar month.

Four of Cups - four months.

Five of Cups - the predicted event may not manifest unless the querent takes speedy action to supervise the particular personalities involved.

Six of Cups - six months.

Seven of Cups - within seven months.

Eight of Cups - a change of heart on the part of the querent may change the predicted outcome.

Nine of Cups - within 48 hours.
Ten of Cups - one month.
Knight of Cups - seven weeks.
Queen of Cups - three months.
Prince of Cups - two months.
Princess of Cups - one month.

Ace of Swords - within one year.

The other Sword cards, from Two to Seven follow this pattern, thus the Two of Swords is within two years, the Seven of Swords within seven years etc..

Eight of Swords - within one year.
Nine of Swords - within two years.
Ten of Swords - within three years.
Knight of Swords - within two years.
Queen of Swords - within three years.

The Prince and Princess of Swords indicate that the event or some foreshadowing of it will occur within one month, however the event will create repercussions which will effect the individuals' life for many years to come.

Ace of Disks - within one week.

Then the same number of weeks as Disks from Two to Ten. Hence the Six of Disks is six weeks etc..

Knight of Disks - twelve months.
Queen of Disks - nine months.
Prince of Disks - six months.
Princess of Disks - three months.

To use this method, one card should be selected with reference to the given situation and then the time factor ascribed to it should be considered. You may need to select more than one card if there are different strands of events in your reading which may come to pass at different points. Again you may find, by experience,that whilst the majority of this list seems to be accurate there seem to be attributions that just don't fit. No system is writ in stone and if, by intelligent adaptation, you can revise this list to work better in your hands, then go ahead.

The Phases of the Moon

You will have seen from the above list the importance placed on the lunar cycle, especially in the time factors ascribed to the Major Arcana. In fact all magickal cultures take notice of the moon and its' changing faces; from the North American Indians to the Taoists of China.

The movement of the moon describes a natural rhythm of time which affects human emotions just as much as it affects the tides in the sea.

In the Western industrialised world, we live by a manmade time. We have a standard 24 hour day within which we live our lives. We live our lives by numbers; 'When it's 7.00am I must get up, when it's 1.00pm, I go and eat lunch, when it's 5.30pm I return from work', etc.. We have forgotten, for the most part, the fact that we experience a far more important physiological time. In other words, millions of years of evolution have adapted us to react to sunlight, to moonlight, to have eyes which can observe the movement of the stars, and an intellect such that we can plot the direction of sunrise at the solstice, and erect vast stone constructions to indicate this direction (such as Stonehenge). Internally our time is governed by patterns of feeding, relaxation, dreaming, by the pulse of the heart muscle and by the expanding and contracting of the lungs. Time, in the sense of a regimented 'something' measured by (or rather created by) clocks, is illusionary. The only real time is physiological time, a perception of chronological progression which occurs in the unconscious mind and may also be perceived by the conscious.

The phases of the moon affect the flow of blood, tissue salts, endocrine secretions and many other factors in the body (this flux is especially noticeable in the menstrual cycle). It is therefore the case that in magick any questions dealing with time relate not to manmade clocks and periods but rather to the ebbs and flows in the universe (from the changes in daylight, from Summer to Winter, to the shifts in the Pole Star over thousands of years). We, as humans are affected far more deeply by the movement of the moon and sun through their cycle, the movement of breath and blood in our bodies than by any information that a standard clock can give us.

If you have not already done so go back over your diary and compare events, dreams etc., with the phase of the lunar cycle occurring at the time. (If you do not have access to any astronomical tables, use a desk diary as these often contain information on the lunar phase.)

The lunar cycle forms the basis of our modern months (originally 'moon' - months such as 'hunting moon' and 'ice moon' appear in various pre-Christian, European calendars), it is approximately 28 days long.

The moon has four faces (not three as often supposed - see Seeds of Magick to clarify this point). Each phase or tide governs a certain aspect of being - thus:

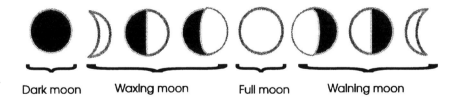

Dark moon   Waxing moon   Full moon   Waning moon

Waxing Moon - growth, new projects, beginnings, developments. Fire of Air

Full Moon - birth, completion, apotheosis of projects, fruition. Fire of Water

Waning Moon - involution, absorption, deconstruction, returning. Earth of Water

Dark Moon - putrefication, preparation, stillness, purification. Earth of Air

As you can see from the above, there are correlations of these phases to four of the sixteen sub-elements. Study this flow; as the movement of the sun (dawn, noon, dusk, midnight) as the menstrual cycle (the pre-ovulatory phase, ovulatory phase, premenstrual phase, menstrual phase), as the flow of the ocean (increasing tide, high- water, ebb tide, low-water), and in many forms until you understand it. Divide a page in your magickal diary into four columns and head each one with a phase of the moon. See if you can find events in your own life (not necessarily occurring over a period of 28 days) which relate to these three tides. Remember these tides are not exactly the same as the elemental classifications but there are major similarities.

Lunar Spread

Cards 1, 2, 3 and 4, are the figurehead cards which determine the lunar phase. Card 1 represents the phase you are in when the reading is done, therefore if the reading is conducted at the full moon then card 2 = waning

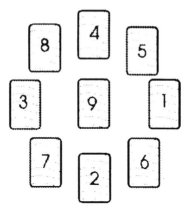

moon, 3 = dark moon and 4 = waxing moon. Cards 5,6,7 and 8 give more information as to how these phases will manifest and card 9 gives an overall feel for the coming month.

The Cycle of the Sun

The same rules apply to the movement of the sun as they do to the moon. Even living in environments which are artificially heated and lit we are still intimately interconnected to the solar cycle through the seasons (even in Equatorial latitudes where the day length is constant, the sun still exhibits different tides in the alternation of plant and animal species). To perform a reading over the course of a year, the simplest method is to use a year/ month spread thus:

Year/ Month Spread

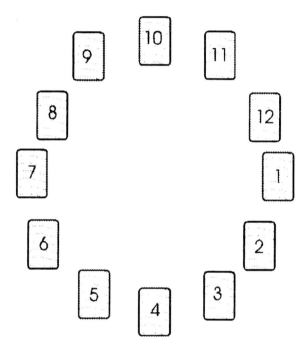

Card 1 is situated in the 'East' of the circle (middle, far right) the direction in which the sun rises. The cards are positioned clockwise to form a circle to follow the way the sun moves in the heavens (in Northern latitudes). Each card then represents a month, so if the reading is being done in June then card 2 is July, 3 = August and so on. Further cards may then be laid out, either on or between the months, to assist in divining the flow of events.

The reading method given above is based on a manmade time system in the months (although the 3651/4 days of the solar cycle is a physiological time period). To divine the course of one year using a more profound method the following spread may be used.

The Year Wheel Spread

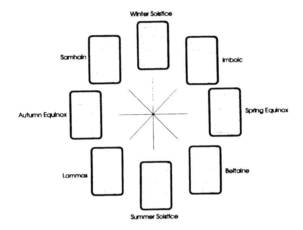

Again the cards are dealt clockwise around the circle, however the first card should be placed at the point in the year where the reading begins (thus, should be reading be done on 4th February then the first card would be placed at point 8 - 'Imbolc'). The four 'cardinal points' (1,3,5 & 7) relate to the Solstices and Equinoxes. That is, the point where the sun is at its' zenith or height (the longest day), its' nadir or depth (the shortest day) and the two Equinoxes where night and daylight are of equal length, one in the Spring, one in the Autumn. The four 'intercardinal' points (2,4,6 & 8) relate to a series of ancient festivals which were (and are) celebrated by many cultures. The timing of these celebrations was based on a complex network of factors; the phases of the moon, agricultural and hunting cycles, stellar cycles etc.. Today, in our chronology of manmade time, these occasions still occur in our calendar. The names given here are of Celtic derivation but you will probably recognise some of the modern variants:

Celtic Name.	Modern Name(s).
Samhain	All Hallows Eve, Halloween, All Souls' Day.
Imbolc	Candlemas,
Beltane	May Day, Labour Day.
Lughnassad	Lammas, Harvest Home, Whitsuntide.

These times are based on physiological chronology and are therefore much more useful in determining the actual flow of events in the life of the querent.

Again, other cards can be laid out to give more information. It is important to stress that in spreads which use physiological time factors, the positions of the cards refer to points in a cycle rather than isolated units in a system. Although the feast of Samhain occurs on October 31st, it is not the day itself which is important but rather the cycle which Samhain represents. The Summer Solstice (the exact date of which is calculated by a celestial movement) is the high point in the solar tide - again the tide is the most important thing - not the date itself. The difference is that which exists between a season, e.g Autumn - which is a tide, and a month, e.g November - which is a limited, convenient way of dividing up the solar cycle into manmade time.

Remember that even by timing an event or change you are still working on probability. Don't be tempted to start predicting the exact date and time of the next stock market crash. The point is to understand the flow of events and help the querent work with and change them as necessary. Trying to pin down events too much simply confuses the intuitional ability. Reading for periods in excess of a year is difficult, as the longer the linear time scale you deal with, the more unknown factors will apply (there is a theory that a tarot card reading cannot predict events more than seven years hence although this is not true in our experience). The main skill of reading is intuitive counselling, the use of any time system is intended to assist this and not to provide a fatalistic and chronologically exact oracle.

Ritual & Reading

Sitting your client down comfortably, offering tea, the use of low lighting and centring exercises - all these practices form a ritualistic procedure. The aim of ritual, in this context, is to provide a method of relaxing and preparing the bodymind of both you and your client. It then serves to focus your attention on the reading, to centre you, and to activate to the fullest all levels of perception you will need. Ritual for reading can thus be defined as have a series of stages.

1) Preparation of space and bodymind.
2) Centreing of self.
3) Stimulation of perceptive ability.
4) Closing.

The way these four sections manifest themselves are detailed below.

The Hermetic Order of the Golden Dawn & Crowley both advocated that a prayer should be said over the cards, prior to their use. Aside of any specifically esoteric implications of this, the prayer serves to focus the mind of the reader on the work at hand. The equivalent would be donning a suit and tie before going to work which is a way of saying 'now I'm putting on my suit and with it a certain persona', the clothes psychologically prepare the individual for a day at the office.

At the close of the reading, another prayer is often advised by occult literature on the Tarot. The effect of this is to form a definite end to the reading, to allow you to return to 'everyday consciousness' (just as the businessman removes his suit at the end of the day to prepare himself for his leisure time).

Ritual, in divination, provides a method of focusing your attention on the act of reading. It can assist both you and the querent in many ways. You may have already adopted, perhaps unknowingly, ritualistic behaviour in your readings. Instances of this include lighting a candle at the beginning of the procedure and extinguishing it at the close. This acts rather like the 'On Air' sign in a television studio - defining the limits of divination. The candle activates the special state of consciousness you have developed when lit and ceremonially terminates it when the candle is snuffed out. You may use the unwrapping of the cards from their wrapping fabric in the same way, ceremonially folding them away after the session. The use of a special reading table, a cloth on which to lay the cards, incense and many other methods may also be used in this fashion. The following are a few methods of reading ritual which follow the four point pattern detailed above. Read through them and perhaps try them out as they stand. In any event, their rationale should be clear. Adapt your own systems and use them.

Simplified Golden Dawn / Crowley Method of Divination Ritual

Prepare your 'working site'. Light candles, if desired, to create a low level of light intensity in the room. Ignite incense if you choose to use to use it.

Hold the deck in the left hand and hold the right hand on top of it. Visualise a sphere of brilliant white light cascading down through your mind and over your body. As it does so, the gates of your intuition are unlocked and the organisational process of your training is evoked.

Say, either aloud or mentally:

"I invoke thee O Unknowable One, that thou wilt send The Word, the great angel which is set over the operations of this secret Wisdom, to lay his hand invisibly upon these consecrated cards of art, that thereby we may obtain true knowledge of hidden things to the glory of thine ineffable Name. Amen."

The cards are then dealt and the reading is done.

To close the reading; square the cards again to form one pile and hold in the right hand. Place the left hand over them and repeat, aloud or silently, the following:

"I thank and exult thee O Word of the Ineffable One that thou hast allowed us to partake of the Wisdom which springs eternally from the Sacred Source of All. Amen"

This time visualise the sphere above your head reabsorbing the white light but remaining brilliant above you. Blow out the candles, extinguish the incense and relax. The symbolism of the prayers given here (shorn of the Hebrew names of God which are included in the original) is that of 'the divine', however this is conceived of, flowing into the reading as a whole and then withdrawing but remaining present in its 'unextended' state after the work is done. The 'Word' spoken of is the active aspect of the elemental matrix of Spirit. It is identical to the 'Word of God' which is a common mythical theme in magick. In psychological terms, the Word could be seen as your own words which have been inspired by the power of your unconscious intuition.

Thoth & The Tarot

The Egyptian god Thoth is described in that mythology as being the deity who presides over divination, speech, writing, recording and measurement. He is depicted as an Ibis headed man, often holding a roll of papyrus and a pen, in his aspect of sacred scribe. Today the Tarot is often said to have been created by Thoth. This does not mean that he actually invented the tarot but rather that the aspects within humanity, which are glyphed by this god, are responsible for the evolution of the tarot. The following ritual uses Thoth and symbolism associated with him to put the reader in the right state of mind. Much as a Catholic Christian would appeal to a specific saint to assist in a particular aspect of their life.

Prepare your room as you wish. Place two candles on either side of your reading table, these should be coloured orange and purple (colours related to Thoth). Light incense if desired (if possible this should be of a light 'airy' scent such as white sandalwood, mastic, myrrh or lemon). Place your deck on the table and light the candles. Imagine the god Thoth standing behind you. You need not visualise this but it is important to feel the presence of this force. One of Thoths' hands rests upon your tarot deck and the other on the nape of your neck. Allow yourself to feel the power emanated by the God passing into you and your deck, take a few moments to relax and feel the energy flowing thorough you. Begin the reading, clear in the knowledge that your intuition will flow smoothly.

After the reading has ended, sit for a few moments with one hand resting on your cards. Imagine again, the god Thoth behind you. This time he turns and walks away, feel him disappearing behind you into the darkness of your subconscious, yet ready to return when you 'will' it. Extinguish first the orange and purple candles and then any other light or incense. Switch on your electric lights, relax and return to 'everyday' consciousness.

Both the examples above involve angels or gods. There is no reason why you could not omit such images but they are potent, even if you only understand them as psychological symbols, and are well worth experimenting with.

Reading Without Pictures

It is perfectly possible to read using cards with little or no pictorial imagery if your intuition has been trained. Try the following exercises. Again don't be afraid to get things 'wrong' but record all your results and just allow the natural process of intuitive insight to happen.

Selecting Cards 'Blind'
Take your deck to your quiet room and relax your bodymind complex. Take the first card, face down, from the top of the pile (shuffle them before hand if necessary).

Try to ascertain which card it is. Record your 'guess' and then look at the card. You should be able to ascertain the elemental and general feel of the card, even if you don't immediately 'know' which card it is. You may find that you call a card incorrectly but name one which has a similar nature: for instance it would not be a complete error to 'guess' a card as being Atu XVIII 'The Moon' when, in fact, it is the Queen of Cups, or 'guessing' Atu XXI 'The Universe' when it is The Ace of Disks. See how many you get correct, how many you are close on and how many totally wrong. Try this experiment often. The better your intuition and knowledge of how your own deck feels, the more accurate you will be. (Bear in mind that you will get at least some cards correct or 'near the mark', by the 'law of averages' alone. Don't get concerned with such statistical probabilities but concentrate on the exercise itself.)

Reading 'Through the Back'
Try this exercise by yourself, then experiment with volunteers using the cards but without turning them face uppermost. This practice is easier than you might expect. After the reading, turn over the cards and see if the overall deal has reflected your reading. Remember that even when reading with the cards face upward the most important thing is not 'the Nine of Swords means...' but rather the flow of the whole reading and the relationships between the cards. Ironically you may, eventually, find that you don't actually need the tarot at all to do a reading.

⊕ - The Eleventh Hour

This chapter provides you with a last opportunity, in the context of this training programme, to cast a retrospective glance at your work. In this chapter, we will suggest a short selection of exercises and revision practices. We have also included a brief discussion of the nature of time.

Re-vision

Looking Forward to Look Back.

Read through all the entries in your magickal record over the whole period that you have been using this book. Now take a sheet of paper and list out the following:

What major questions do you still lack answers to?

How do you propose to answer them?

What do you want to accomplish over the next few months? (Include in this financial, personal as well as 'esoteric' goals.)

Has the tarot provided you with an effective framework in which to work?

What other frameworks could you, or would you like to use?

What changes have you experienced in your own life?

What changes do you expect to happen to you in the next few months?

Write down your answers to these, and any other questions that come to mind. Slip the sheet of paper into your magickal diary, refer to it after two months have elapsed.

Quiet Survey

Unless you have moved house or been able to work in numerous locations, you will have done a number of exercises in your own 'quiet room'. Go into your quiet room and consider the following questions: How has the physical layout of your room changed over the course of your studies? Have these physical changes mirrored other changes happening inside of you? Has the atmosphere in your quiet room become significantly different from the rest of the house?

Are other people aware of any different atmosphere in your quiet room?

If you have used you room for any sort of ritual work, has this affected

178

its' atmosphere? What other locations have the same feel as this place?

Others En Route

In the course of your training, using this manual, you will probably have had contact with numerous other people in various walks of life, and on many different levels. (If you are studying divination, don't forget to include people you have read for.) Using your record as reference, list some of the people you have met over the last few weeks. Consider the following points with relation to all of them.

Why were these people part of my life?

What did I, or could I have learnt from these people?

What did I teach them?

How do they relate to me now?

The second and third questions in this list are most important. In Buddhism, it is said that everyone carries the spark of Buddhahood within and could very well be a boddisatva (enlightened one) 'in disguise'.

Meditation

Go to your quiet room. Relax your bodymind (you may wish to do a centring exercise such as the Cross of Powers to help).

Imagine that you are sitting on a hill under the open sky. About you throng all the people in the world. The air is hushed and still - they are waiting for you to speak words of wisdom, to show them what you have learned, and what you would bid them do for themselves.

Stay with this imagined situation for a while. What would you say? Would you say anything? How could you explain a potentially complex series of ideas to so many people? If your ideas are founded on experience, how could you advise humanity to live to gain this experience?

If you wish to say anything, or make any kind of statement to the imagined crowd, do so. Remember that, following the principle of the macro/microcosm, each of these people could be seen as part of yourself. Relax and let the imagined scenario fade.

The Nature of Time

Whether you have been following the divination or self exploration pathways through this book, you will notice that the esoteric view of time is radically different from the exoteric view. Essentially, we all perceive linear time, we measure this by the vibration in quartz crystals (in digital watches), to the progression of the Wednesday to Thursday (in the Christian calendar). Yet since the advent of Einsteins' special theory of relativity, and the emergence of psychology as an accepted science, we have seen our perception of time change. Einstein, and the quantum physicists have shown that the apparent flow of time is not a universal constant. If we take two atomic clocks, which are exactly synchronised, it is possible to show that the flow of time changes. One atomic clock is kept on the ground, the other is placed in a jet plane and flown at high speed, high in the atmosphere. When the clocks are returned together there is a noticeable time lag on the clock that has been in the jet. Both the clock and the crew of the jet plane have experienced time flowing more 'slowly' than those stationary on the ground. On a psychological level, time appears to pass much more slowly for the artists' human model than it does for the artist at her canvas. Until recently it was supposed that the speed of light provided a universal constant; that is a yardstick of time. It was thought that the speed of light was the fastest that anything could travel, and thus gave a natural ceiling to all change in the universe. But modern physics, dealing with sub-atomic particles, black holes and the like, has disproved this. It seems we live in a universe of quality, far more than of Newtonian quantity - in fact particulate physics has started adopting very 'magickal' terminology for its own observations. Some scientists are suggesting that matter is the function of four qualities named 'truth', 'beauty', 'strangeness' & 'charm'.

The essential point of this is that, even modern science (which is still backward in many of its' methods and theorems) disputes the apparent flow of linear time.

In magickal theory there is no assumption that time flows like a river inexorably one way, from source to the sea. Rather it is like the hydrostatic cycle taken as whole - without beginning or end.

Without complicating the issue, the esoteric view of time may be described by the following diagram.

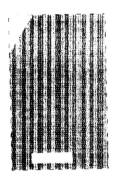

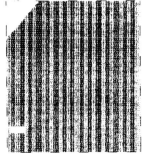

Time spirals upward, in an unending cycle of change. As the spiral moves 'upwards', events repeat themselves at a 'higher level'. To take a simple, human, example the: First World War occurred in 1914 to 1918. The progression of events then followed the curve of the spiral, in this diagram, until it reached the identical point in the next level of the spiral, the Second World War. This is just an example and does not mean that each loop in the spiral is 25 years (1914 to 1939) long. Time is not a line but a cycle.

At a still more profound level, the only actual time is 'now'. The question 'do your friends still exist even when you don't have them with you?', is a valid one. Even in physics it is becoming apparent that perception is the key to the universe.

Time itself may be an illusion; or rather it does not exist unless we perceive it as 'real'. Having said that, it is a very useful illusion, for planning dinner engagements : however the bars of linear time are thin and easily broken. It is perception of time, be it from different places

181

(such as in a jet plane), psychological state (such as being an artists model), or level of reality (such as being a trance state or ritual situation) that matters.

- The Tarot into Tomorrow

If you have followed the course of work set out in this book then you will have made a good start in answering the question we posed in the first hexagram chapter: 'Who are you?'

The studies, exercises and concepts detailed in this book are just a start, there are more things in heaven and earth than even the most lofty magickians have dreamt of. Having covered the work in this text, give yourself a mental pat on the back for such discipline, foolhardiness, bravery, organisation and for surviving, we suspect, at least a couple of sleepless nights.

So where do you go from here? The choice is up to your conscious mind and True Will. The 'further reading' section in the bibliography could give you some ideas, or you may wish to get in contact, if you haven't done so yet with other like-minded folk (be warned that, not to put too fine a point on it, there are plenty of lunatics, charlatans and self-appointed magi out there in the 'magickal community').

Wherever you go we wish you well. Should you wish to contact us you may do so via the publishers - we do make every effort to reply to any letters we get and would very much like to hear from you.

Like the Fool who carries the Ten of Disks with him when he begins his journey, you have all you need with you now. It's just a matter of becoming aware of it.

This is not the end of the Book, just the beginning...

☆Pentagram - Into The Mystery

Having worked through the divination orientated path in this book we would like to congratulate you. Divination is one of the most difficult occult skills to develop, even with the most vigorous study and practice of the things taught in this book, it will take years for you to become a truly excellent reader. This is not a defect in the exercises or methods given here, nor in the individual student - it is simply that reading the cards necessitates experience, this is the real key to learning in any field, and especially in magick.

Should we have sufficiently wetted your appetite for more of magick we would suggest that you take at least three months off to look back at your own work and, more importantly, to really use the skills you have gained. Don't concentrate all your attention on that which is specifically 'esoteric' or 'mystical' - if you develop the right attitude and perception, there is as much magickal understanding to be gained out of digging the garden as pouring over the texts of Aleister Crowley et al. After your break, you may wish to begin again and follow the Hexagram path through this book. You may also wish to examine the books detailed in the further reading list in the bibliography and perhaps make contact with others who share your interest.

We would very much like to hear from you, so if you want to contact us, either to discuss matters concerned with this book, magick as a whole or just for a chat, write care of the publisher.

We wish you well in the future, present and past.

Bibliography

The following texts have been divided into sections determined by the major aspects of magick covered by each book. You should try to gain as great an exposure to ideas in different media as possible. We have included a brief list of recordings that you might find suitable for some of the practices in this book. Should you have any problems then try ordering books from your local library, or contact the suppliers listed on the previous pages. From the perspective of the issues covered in this book, and to reflect what we feel is the all round accuracy and value of the texts, each book is 'graded' thus:

    **** = Indicates 'vital' reading.
    ***   = indicates highly recommended.
    **   = indicates recommended.
    *   = indicates suggested.

Texts about magick covering various areas. Carroll, Pete, liber Null, Morton Press, 1987. ***
Crowley, Aleister, Magick, Routledge & Kegan Paul, 1983.****
Conway, David, Magic. An Occult Primer, Mayflower Books, 1976.**
Cavendish, Richard (editor), The Encyclopedia of The Unexplained, Routledge & Kegan Paul, 1974.***
Hine, Phil, Walking Between The Worlds, Pagan News Publications, 1989.*
Valiente, Doreen, Witchcraft for Tomorrow, Hale, 1978. ****

Texts about bodymind disciplines.
Coster, G., Yoga and Western Psychology, Oxford University Press, 1950.*
Dunne, Desmond, Yoga for Everyone, New English Library, 1970.***
Richmond, S., Common Sense About Yoga, MacGibbon & Kee, 1971.**
Scott, Mary, Kundalini in the Physical World, Routledge & Kegan Paul, 1983.*
Yu, L.K., The Secrets of Chinese Meditation, Rider, 1969.*

Texts about mythology & belief systems.
Campbell, Joseph, The Masks of God: Primitive Mythology, Penguin Books, 1984.****
Asswyn, Freya, The Leaves of Yggdrasill, Llewellyn, 1990. **
Deren, Maya, The Voodoo Gods, Granada, 1975.*
Frazer, James G., The Golden Bough, Macmillan Press, 1978.****
Seligman, Kurt, Magic, Supernaturalism and Religion, Granada, 1975.*
Wallis-Budge, E.A, The Book of The Dead, Arkana, 1985.**
Warner, Rex (forward), Encyclopedia of World Mythology, Peerage Books, 1975.****
Various, The Holy Books of Thelema, Samuel Weiser, 1983.**

Texts devoted to the study of the tarot.

Tarot - The Complete Guide, Cynthia Giles, 1992 ****
Crowley, Aleister, The Book of Thoth, Samuel Weiser, 1980.***
Nichols, Sallie, Jung and Tarot, Samuel Weiser, 1980.**
Roberts, Richard, Tarot & You, Morgan & Morgan, 1975.**
Kaplan, Stuart R., The Encyclopedia of Tarot, U.S.Games Systems, 1978.***
Bridges, Carol, The Medicine Woman Inner Guidebook, Earth Nation Publishing, 1987.**
Peach, Emily, The Tarot Workbook, Aquarian Press, 1984.*
Summers, Catherine & Vayne, Julian, Self-Development with the Tarot, Foulsham, 1992. ***

Texts dealing with psychology and related topics.
Inglis, Brian, Trance, Collins, 1989.***
Mindell, Arnold, Dreambody, Routledge & Kegan Paul, 1984.***
Lusher, Max, Lucher Colour Test, Pan Books, 1972.*
Jung, Carl.G, Man and His Symbols, Pan Books, 1978.**
Von Franz, Marie-Louise, On Dreams & Death, Shambhala, 1986.**

Texts devoted to the Qabalah and related matters.
Halevi, Z'ev ben Shimon, Kabbalah, Thames and Hudson, 1988.***
Ashcroft-Norwicki, The Shining Paths, Aquarian Press, 1983.*
Highfield, A.C., The Book of Celestial Images, Aquarian Press, 1984.****
Parfitt, Will, The Qabalah, Element, 1991. ****
Crowley, Aleister, 777 and Other Qabalistic Writings, Samuel Wesier, 1982.****
Mathers, S.L.M. (editor & translator), Kabbalah Unveiled: The Books of the Zohar, Routledge & Kegan Paul, 1970.*
Regardie, Israel, A Garden of Pomegranates, Llewellyn, 1978.**

Miscellaneous and other divination methods.
Bord, Janet & Colin, Earth Rites, Granada, 1982.***
Butler, W.B., How to Read the Aura, Aquarian Press, 1982.*
Eliot, T.S., Selected Poems, Faber & Faber, 1969.***
Oken, Alan, Complete Astrology, Bantum, 1980.****
Over, Raymond Van (editor), I Ching, Mentor Books, 1971.**
Shuttle, Penelope & Redgrove, Peter, The Wise Wound, Paladin, 1986. ****
Vinci, Leo, Incense, Aquarian Press, 1980.***
Farrar, Janet & Stewart, The Witches' Way, Robert Hale, 1984.**
Starhawk, Truth or Dare, Harper & Row, 1990. ****
Douglas, Nik & Slinger, Penny, Sexual Secrets, Arrow Books, 1982.**

Qabalistic Key Scale Correspondences

The Following Listing is based on the Golden Dawn/Crowley attributions of predominant colours ascribed to each Sephira and Path on the Tree of Life. The 'Key Numbers' given on the far left column are common to the reference system found in Crowley's' 777 & The Book of Thoth. Each number relates to a path, and therefore an Atu, in the Qabalah (numbers of each path are given in the diagram of the Tree of Life page XXX). The Second set of numbers, 1 to 10, give colours ascribed to each Sephira (again numbered as per the diagram). Each colour is described as being of the Knight Scale, Queen Scale, Prince Scale or Princess Scale (i.e the different elemental facets of each path/sephira).

No	Sephira	Knight	Queen	Prince	Princess
1	Kether	brilliance	white brilliance	white brilliance	white flecked gold
2	Chokmah	pure soft blue	grey	blue pearl grey like mother of pearl	white flecked red, blue and yellow
3	Binah	crimson	black	dark brown	grey flecked pink
4	Chesed	deep violent	blue	deep purple	deep azure, flecked yellow
5	Geburah	orange	scarlet red	bright scarlet	red flecked black
6	Tiphereth	clear pink rose	yellow (gold)	rich salmon	gold amber
7	Netzach	amber	emerald	bright yellow green	olive flecked gold
8	Hod	violet	orange	red-russet	yellowish-brown flecked white
9	Yesod	indigo	violet	very dark purple	citrine flecked azure
10	Malkuth	yellow	citrine(N), olive (E), russet(W) & Black(S)	as Queen but gold flecked black	black rayed with yellow

Atu	path no	Knight	Queen	Prince	Princess
0	11	bright pale blue	sky blue	blue emerald green	emerald flecked gold
I	12	yellow	purple	grey	indigo rayed violet
II	13	blue	silver	cold pale blue	silver rayed sky blue
III	14	emerald green	sky blue	early spring green rayed pale green	bright rose or cerise
IV	15	scarlet	red	brilliant flame	glowing red
V	16	red	orange	deep indigo	deep warm olive rich brown
VI	17	orange	pale mauve	new yellow leather	reddish grey inclined to mauve
VII	18	amber	maroon	rich bright russet	dark greenish brown
VIII	19	yellow (greenish)	deep purple	grey	reddish amber
IX	20	green (yellowish)	slate grey	green grey	plum colour
X	21	violet	blue	rich purple	bright blue rayed yellow
XI	22	emerald green	blue	deep blue-green pale	green
XII	23	deep blue	sea-green	deep olive-green	white flecked purple
XIII	24	green blue	dull brown	very dark brown	livid indigo brown
XIV	25	blue	yellow	green	dark vivid blue
XV	26	indigo	black	blue-black	cold dark grey nearing black
XVI	27	scarlet	red	venetian red	bright red rayed azure or emerald
XVII	28	violet	sky blue	bluish mauve	white tinged purple
XVIII	29	crimson	buff flecked (ultra violet)	light translucent stone silver white	colour pinkish brown
XIX	30	orange	gold yellow	rich amber	amber rayed red
XX	31	glowing orange scarlet	vermilion	scarlet flecked gold	vermilion flecked crimson and emerald
XXI	32	indigo	black	blue-black	black rayed blue

A selection of other titles from Capall Bann:

Available through your local bookshop, or direct from Capall Bann at: Freshfields, Chieveley, Berks, RG16 8TF.

West Country Wicca - A Journal of the Old Religion By Rhiannon Ryall

This book is a valuable and enjoyable contribution to contemporary Wicca. It is a simple account of the Old Religion. The portrayal of Wicca in the olden days is at once charming and deeply religious, combining joy, simplicity and reverence. The wisdom emanating from country folk who live close to Nature shines forth from every page - a wisdom which can add depth and colour to our present day understanding of the Craft. Without placing more value on her way than ours, Rhiannon provides us with a direct path back to the Old Religion in the British Isles. *This is how it was*, she tells us. *This is the way I remember it.* Both the content of what she remembers and the form in which she tells us, are straightforward, homespun and thoroughly unaffected.

"West Country Wicca is a real gem - it is the best book on witchcraft I have ever seen! Thank you Rhiannon Ryall for sharing your path with us." - Marion Weinstein

ISBN Number   1 89830 702 4   Price £7.95

The Call of the Horned Piper by Nigel Aldcroft Jackson

This book originated as a series of articles, later much expanded, covering the symbolism, archetypes and myths of the Traditional Craft (or Old Religion) in the British Isles and Europe. The first section of the book explores the inner symbology and mythopoetics of the old Witchraft religion, whilst the second part gives a practical treatment of the sacred sabbatic cycle, the working tools, incantations, spells and pathworking. There are also sections on spirit lines, knots and thread lore and ancestral faery teachings. Extensively illustrated with the author's original artwork. This is a radical and fresh re-appraisal of authentic witch-lore which may provide a working alternative to current mainstream trends in Wicca.

ISBN Number   1-898307-09-1   Price £8.95

The Sacred Grove - The Mysteries of the Tree By Yvonne Aburrow

The veneration of trees was a predominant theme in the paganism of the Romans, Greeks, Celtic & Germanic peoples. Many of their rites took place in sacred groves & much of their symbolism involved the cosmic tree; its branches supported the heavens, its trunk was the centre of the earth & its roots penetrated the underworld. This book explains the various mysteries of the tree & explains how these can be incorporated into modern paganism. This gives a new perspective on the cycle of seasonal festivals & the book includes a series of rituals incorporating tree symbolism. "The Sacred Grove" is the companion volume to "The Enchanted Forest - The Magical Lore of Trees, but can be read in its own right as an exploration of the mysteries of the tree.

ISBN Number 1 898307 12 1   Price £10.95

Angels & Goddesses - Celtic Paganism & Christianity
by Michael Howard

This book traces the history and development of Celtic Paganism and Celtic Christianity specifically in Wales, but also in relation to the rest of the British Isles including Ireland, during the period from the Iron Age, through to the present day. It also studies the transition between the old pagan religions & Christianity & how the early Church, especially in the Celtic counmtries, both struggled with & later absorbed the earlier forms of spirituality it encountered. The book also deals with the way in which the Roman Catholic version of Christianity arrived in south-east England & the end of the 6th century, when the Pope sent St. Augustine on his famous mission to convert the pagan Saxons, & how this affected the Celtic Church.. It discusses how the Roman Church suppressed Celtic Christianity & the effect this was to have on the history & theology of the Church during the later Middle Ages. The influence of Celtic Chhristianity on the Arthurian legends & the Grail romances is explored as well as surviving traditions of Celtic bardism in the medieval period. The conclusion on the book covers the interest in Celtic Christianity today & how, despite attempts to eradicate it from the pages of clerical history, its ideas & ideals have managed to survive & are now influencing New Age concepts & are relevent to the critical debate about the future of the modern chrurch.

ISBN 1-898307-03-2 Price £9.95

Auguries and Omens - The Magical Lore of Birds By Yvonne Aburrow

The folklore & mythology of birds is central to an understanding of the ancient world, yet it is a neglected topic. This book sets out to remedy this situation, examining in detail the interpretation of birds as auguries & omens, the mythology of birds (Roman, Greek, Celtic & Teutonic), the folklore & weather lore associated with them, their use in heraldry & falconry & their appearances in folk songs & poetry. The book examines these areas in a general way, then goes into specific details of individual birds from the albatross to the yellowhammer, including many indigenous British species, as well as more exotic & even mythical birds.

ISBN Number 1 898307 11 3   Price £10.95

The Pickingill Papers - The Origin of the Gardnerian Craft by W. E. Liddell
Compiled & Edited by Michael Howard

George Pickingill (1816 - 1909) was said to be the leader of the witches in Canewdon, Essex. In detailed correspondence with 'The Wiccan' & 'The Cauldron' magazines from 1974 - 1994, E. W. Liddell, claimed to be a member of the Hereditary Craft. He further claimed that he had relatives in various parts of southern England who were coven leaders & that his own parent coven had been founded by George Pickingill's grandfather in the 18th century. There is considerable interest in the material in the so-called 'Pickingill Papers' & the controversy still rages about their content & significance with regard to the origins of Gardnerian Wicca. This book provides, for the first time, a chance for the complete Pickingill material to be read & examined in toto together with background references & extensive explanatory notes. Topics include the origin of the Gardnerian Book of Shadows & Aleister Crowley's involvement, the relationship between the Hereditary Craft, Gardnerian Wicca & Pickingill's Nine Covens, the influence of Freemasonry on the medieval witch cult, sex magic, ley lines & earth energy, prehistoric shamanism and the East Anglian lodges of cunning men. It also includes new material on the Craft Laws, the New Forest coven & Pickingill's influence on the Revived Craft.

ISBN Number 1 898307 10 5   Price £9.95

The Witches of Oz By Matthew & Julia Philips

This is a well thought-out & highly practical guide to Wicca, the Old Religion. The authors run a modern Wiccan coven based on a blend of Gardnerian & Alexandrian ritual. The book starts by answering the question 'What is Wicca?' in simple, straightforward terms. A brief explanation of the history of modern Wicca is given, the authors then go on to describe the working tools used in Wicca, the festivals, special celebrations - Handfasting (marriage), Wiccaning & a Requiem, how to set up a circle, the philosophy & ethics of magic & how to work it. There are also sections on children in Wicca, incense, suitable recipes & spells. What makes this book different from many others written on the subject is the practical no-nonsense advice & the straightforward explanations of what is done & why. As readers may guess from the title, the authors live in Australia, though Julia originally came from England. Of course the rites & information given apply equally to the northern & southern hemispheres. Julia Philips is the editor of the internationally respected magazine 'Web of Wyrd'.

Price £8.95   ISBN 1 898307 180

Pathworking 2nd Ed. By Pete Jennings & Pete Sawyer

A pathworking is, very simply, a guided meditational exercise, it is sometimes referred to as 'channelling' or 'questing'. It is used for many different aims, from raising consciousness to healing rituals You don't have to possess particular beliefs or large sums of money to benefit from it & it can be conducted within a group or solo at time intervals to suit you. This book teaches you how to alter your conscious state, deal with stress, search for esoteric knowledge or simply have fun & relax. It starts with a clear explanation of the theory of pathworking and shows in simple & concise terms what it is about and how to achieve results, then goes on to more advanced paths & how to develop your own, it also contains over 30 detailed and explained pathworkings. Highly practical advice & information is given on how to establish and manage your own group. No previous experience is assumed.

ISBN Number   1 898307 00 8   Price £7.95

Celtic Lore & Druidic Ritual By Rhiannon Ryall

Rhiannon Ryall is well known for her book 'West Country Wicca'. This new book brings some of the inner mysteries to those interested in the Pagan Path or Tradition. Inevitably the Druidic Path crosses that of any genuine Gaelic Tradition of Wicca, so this book contains much druidic lore.. Background material pertaining to the Druids is also included as this explains much of their way of viewing the world and it enables the reader to understand more fully their attributions in general and their rituals in particular. The book is divided into five parts:

1: Casting circles, seasonal sigils, wands, woods for times of the year, Celtic runes, the Great Tides, making cones and vortices, polarities and how to change them, the seasonal Ogham keys and some Ogham correspondences. 2: Old calendar festivals and associated evocations, the "Call of Nine", two versions of the 'Six pointed Star Dance', Mistletoe Lore, New Moon working,the Fivefold Calendar. 3: Underlying fundamentals of magical work, magical squares and their applications, more use of Oghams, the Diamond Working area. 4: Five initiations, including a shamanic one, some minor 'calls', some 'little magics'. 5: Background information on the Celtic path, the Arthurian myth and its underlying meaning and significance, the Three Worlds of the Celts, thoughts regarding the Hidden Path, some thoughts and final advice. A veritable treasure trove for anyone interested in the Celtic path.

ISBN 1 898307 225   Price £9.95

The Mysteries of the Runes By Michael Howard

The book follows the historical development of the runes from earlier Neolithic & Bronze Age alphabets & symbols & their connection with other magical & mystical symbols including the swastika, sunwheel, equal-armed cross etc. Historical references to the runes & their use in divination by Germanic tribes & the Saxons together with the Viking use of the runes in Dark Age Engl& are also covered. The Norse god Odin is discussed, as the shaman-god of the runes together with his associated myths, legends & folklore, the Wild Hunt, the Valkyries & his connections with the Roman god Mercury, the Egyptian god Thoth, Jesus & the Odinic mysteries. The magical uses of the runes are described, their use in divination with examples of their everyday use. Fascinating information is included on the runes discovered during archaelogical excavations, rune masters & mistresses, the bog sacrifices of Sc&anavia & the training of the rune master, both ancient & modern.

The symbolism and detailed descriptions of each of the eight runes of Freya's Aett, Haegl's Aett & Tyr's Aett are given with divinity, religious symbolism & spiritual meanings etc based on The Anglo Saxon Rune Poem. Details on how to make your own set of runes are included, how to cast the runes for divination with examples of readings &suggested layouts & the use of rune magic. The final section covers Bronze Age Sc&anavia & its religious belief systems; the gods & goddess of the Aesir & Vanir, their myths & legends & the seasonal cycle of festivals in the Northern Tradition. Also discussed are the Web of Wyrd & the Norns, Saxon/Norse paganism & traditional witchcraft.

ISBN Number   1-898307-07-0   Price £8.95

The Enchanted Forest - The Magical Lore of Trees By Yvonne Aburrow

This is a truly unique book covering the mythology, folklore, medicinal & craft uses of trees. Associated rhymes & songs are also included together with the esoteric correspondences - polarity, planet, deity, rune & Ogham. There is a short history of tree lore, its purpose & applications. A further section gives information on tree spirits & their importance. The text is profusely illustrated with line drawings by the author & artist Gill Bent. This book will appeal to anyone who likes trees.

ISBN Number   1-898307-08-3   Price £10.95

In Search of Herne the Hunter By Eric Fitch

The book commences with an introduction to Herne's story & his relationship with Windsor, the oak on which Herne hanged himself & its significance in history & mythology. The next section investigates antlers & their symbology in prehistoric religions, together with a study of the horned god Cernunnos, the Wild Hunt & its associations with Woden, Herne etc. & the Christian devil. There is a descriptive chapter on the tradition of dressing up as animals & the wearing & use of antlers in particular. Herne's suicide & its connection with Woden & prehistoric sacrifice is covered, together with the most complete collection of Herne's appearances, plus an investigation into the nature of his hauntings. The final section brings all the strands together, plus some additional material. Photographs, illustrations & diagrams enhance the authoritative & well researched text. The book also contains appendices covering the 19th century opera on the legend of Herne, Herne & his status in certain esoteric circles & Herne & Paganism/Wicca.

Price £9.95   ISBN 1 898307 237